YOUR EYES SAW

A mother's journey when
God said no to her
most desperate plea

BRENDA LURTEY

BOOKS

Published by: ADVANTAGE BOOKS™
                 Longwood, Florida, USA
                 www.advbookstore.com

Library of Congress Catalog Number: 2016939198

Credits: Front Cover photo: Christa Rene Photography
        Back Cover photos: David Lurtey, Susan Meyers
        Cover Design: David McQuaid
        Editor: Rebecca Moore

First Printing: May 2016
16 17 18 19 20 21 22   10 9 8 7 6 5 4 3 2 1
Printed in the United States of America

Your Eyes Saw **is dedicated to my precious son, my hero,**

Todd Lurtey

Second Timothy 4:7 can truly be said of you: "I have fought the good fight, I have finished the race, I have kept the faith. Henceforth there is laid up for me the crown of righteousness, which the Lord, the righteous judge, will award to me on that Day, and not only to me but also to all who have loved his appearing."

Brenda Lurtey

Your eyes saw my unformed substance; in your book were written, every one of them, the days that were formed for me, when as yet there were none of them.   Psalm 139:16

Brenda Lurtey

Table of Contents

Preface

Ever since I was a little girl, I have had a secret desire to write a book. There is just one problem: I'm not a writer. In my mind it was just a dream I had to put on a shelf because it would never come to pass.

After my son Todd died, several people sent me messages encouraging me to write his story. I gave everyone the same answer: "I can't; I'm not a writer." From time to time, however, I allowed myself to daydream about what it would be like to actually write out the events surrounding Todd's life and death. In the fall of 2013 I had the opportunity to share Todd's story with two audiologists in Maryland. As I spoke, I remember being surprised at how intently these strangers listened to me and how interested they both seemed in the details I gave them. At the end of our conversation, one of them emphatically said, "You should write a book." I gave him my normal answer. "I can't; I'm not a writer—besides, who would buy it?" His answer was what God used to begin working on my heart. "I would."

I began to pray, *"Lord, is this something I can do? Is this something You want me to do?"* My desire to share what I observed the Lord do in Todd's life became strong, and I decided I would do my part. I would write the details, and the end result would be left up to the Lord.

This book is the fulfillment of a dream I never thought I could accomplish. But it is much more than that; it is a testimony to God's amazing grace in the life of my son. Although I was a part of this journey, it feels as if I was given a front row seat to view an incredible display of God's grace and peace played out in the life of someone I love very dearly.

"Delight yourself in the Lord, and he will give you the desires of your heart." Psalm 37:4

Brenda Lurtey

Special Thanks

To Todd's oncologists, Dr. Anderson, Dr. Bryant, and Dr. Cook— Oncology patients and parents are blessed to have you walk with them on the cancer journey. Thank you from the bottom of my heart for taking such good care of Todd. We will never forget not only your expertise but also your compassion and kindness in caring for him. You will always be a part of our lives. Dr. Anderson, you were the first oncologist I met, and right away I knew there was something special about you. You are truly one of the kindest people I know. The first day you came to Todd's hospital room, you offered us the gift of hope, and you continued to provide that hope throughout Todd's illness. I will always be grateful for you. Dr. Bryant, you could always make me laugh when you came in to check on Todd. Even when his situation was bleak, you would engage us in discussions about normal life. With all of the serious issues cancer patients have to face, they definitely need humor and laughter. We are grateful for your professional manner and for the joy you gave us. Dr. Cook, you were always so sweet. I could see worry in your eyes on many occasions, but you always looked at Todd with compassion and spoke so kindly to him. You were also gentle and kind to me. I remember so well your offering me a hug at the clinic when we knew Todd's situation was bleak. Although you have the professionalism of a doctor, you have the heart of a mother.

To Dr. Chandler—Thank you for your expert care of Todd throughout all of his surgical procedures. You took care of him when I was powerless to help him, and I will never forget that. I always felt sad for you—you were the one who had to deliver bad news to me so often, but I am grateful that it was always delivered with compassion. You started out as a stranger, and now we are blessed to call you a friend. Thank you for remaining a part of our lives and for letting us be a part of yours. You held a special place in Todd's heart, and you hold a special place in our heart. We consider your family a part of our family.

To Todd's sweet nurses—You guys are amazing! Your ease among the patients and your knowledge of all the chemo medicines are remarkable. The job of a pediatric cancer floor nurse has to be very difficult—not only physically, but also emotionally. You take care of our children, yet you take care of the parents too! Many times I cried with you all and I was always offered a hug. I often observed that when the cancer patients were having a bad day, you kept your emotions on an even level and offered them comfort and hope. I hold you close in my heart and will never forget the fact that you lovingly took care of my son. He loved you, and so do I.

To Amy Bowers—You were one of the first people I met from the children's oncology floor. Your cheerful disposition and warm personality made me instantly like you, but I grew to have a great love and respect for you as you interacted with Todd and me. You really do go above and beyond to make sure your cancer kids' needs are being met—and not just their needs, but the needs of the parents as well. I'm so glad you are still in our lives. Thank you for all the love and support you continue to provide for our family.

To "Charlie Pops"—I will never forget the first day you met Todd and told him your name is Charlie. Todd said, "I think I will call you Pops." That name is indicative of the bond the two of you shared. Thank you for the love and care you show to all of your oncology kids. You have a heart of gold, and I am so thankful for the joy you brought into our lives everyday we were in the hospital. To me, you are an unsung hero. But God sees all you do for the children, and that is what counts.

To Pastor Danny—Your life has been an amazing example to our family, and especially to me, of someone who walks with God. Thank you for always being with our family through various trials and illnesses. We appreciate the many times you woke up early to come to the hospital and pray with one of us before various surgeries. Your presence was always a comfort to us and your prayers were and are powerful. We are honored and blessed to call you our pastor and our friend. Todd loved you, and so do we.

To Todd's classmates, the class of 2016—Todd never really expressed sadness that he had cancer, but his one regret was that he couldn't be with you all. Some of you he had known since infant nursery. Thank you so much for your prayers for him and for the support you gave him throughout his illness. I will never forget the day Connor brought the video you all had made for Todd. He hadn't smiled much, but when he saw your faces and heard your greetings, his famous smile stretched from ear to ear. As you graduate, I know he would want to tell you to live for God for the rest of your lives. In the end, it's all that matters—as Todd now knows better than we!

To Brandon, Lauren, and Jeffrey—I love you all very much and am so thankful to be your mom. I know losing your brother was difficult, and living without him is sad, but Dad and I are so proud of the way you respond to your grief. My heart is blessed by how you all lovingly comfort me when you see tears running down my cheeks. Your compassion and strength have been amazing. I can't wait to see all four of you together again one day. What a wonderful reunion it will be!

To David—Although we dedicated Todd to the Lord as an infant, I don't think either one of us ever dreamed of a future day when God would actually ask us for such a sacrifice as to walk with Todd through the valley of the shadow of death and to hand him back to the Lord. In this journey of grief, one of the things I love the most about you is that you have never seemed annoyed by my tears. You have always wrapped your arms around me and offered your comfort—even though it was your loss as well as mine. It is a blessing that on the days I am struggling, you are strong; and on the days I see your chin quivering, I am strong—well, maybe not totally strong—but let's just say on that particular day, I may be doing better than usual. I'm thankful God brought this Canadian girl and her Indiana boy together many years ago. You were worth the wait!

Introduction

From before the beginning of time, God knew my second child, Todd, would be born at 11:50 a.m. on March 4, 1997, and He knew Todd would die at 9:20 p.m. on May 10, 2013. That was God's plan.

I also had a plan for Todd's life. My plan was for him to have a happy childhood, accept Christ as his Savior at an early age, grow up, get married, and have children of his own. He would live a long, healthy, and happy life. My plans were good; in my mind, they were noble plans.

I did not plan for him to be born with a genetic disease. I did not plan for him to get cancer just as he started his freshman year of high school. I certainly did not plan for him to die when he had just turned sixteen. Todd had so much more to do on this earth, things I wanted him to do. In essence, I wrote my own story for his life. Looking back, I know I wanted the Lord's input, but without realizing it, I was not allowing Him to be the author of Todd's life story.

To say the least, the way Todd's story ended disappointed me profoundly. God disappointed me. He was not who I thought He was. As I saw it, He let me down. While Todd fought cancer, well-meaning Christians assured me that all I had to do was believe God would heal Todd, and He would. I just had to have faith. Trust me; I tried with all my might to have faith. I willed everything in me to believe God would heal Todd.

In the end, nothing worked. Cancer took Todd's life, just as—I am sure—nearly everyone assumed it would. I am a child of God; I expected more from Him. I expected a miracle. I didn't necessarily think we deserved a miracle, but I believed that if I had enough faith, God's natural response would be to heal Todd miraculously. How would God receive any glory if Todd died just as people anticipated? Where was the miracle I prayed for, that literally thousands of people across the world prayed for? Wasn't it true that God would be glorified if He healed Todd? Hadn't I prayed and revealed my wishes to the Lord? My plan was simple: God heals Todd; God receives the glory. To paint a picture of my thought process, God was in my football huddle, but I was calling the plays.

With each new challenge to Todd's health, our anticipated outcome grew bleaker. It took more and more effort on my part, but after each setback, I developed a new strategy for Todd's care and presented it to the Lord for His implementation. It's a good thing He got my input, because He really needed it, right? I informed the Creator of the universe what was best for my child! The Lord had a lot to teach me regarding my plans and His plans. His lesson would be one of the hardest of my life.

As I sat in the front row of our church staring up at the pulpit, I thought back to Todd's baby dedication service just sixteen short years earlier when our pastor, Danny, prayed for Todd for the first time.

I want to ask David and Brenda Lurtey to come at this time with their son. We want to introduce to you Todd Frederick James Lurtey. He was born March 4, and the Lurteys have asked that we have a prayer of dedication. Would you join me, please, as we have a prayer of dedication for David and Brenda, and also for Todd?

Heavenly Father, we rejoice in your graciousness and give You thanks that You are a loving and good Heavenly Father, that it is Your heart's intent to bless us abundantly above all that we could ask or think. And it gives us great confidence as we come to You this morning because we confess that we are often not even sure of how we should pray. And yet, You interpret those prayers and do not answer them strictly as we ask them, but You answer them above and beyond what we ask or think. And so our prayer this morning is turned in behalf of David and Brenda, that You would give them great skill and wisdom as parents, compassion of heart, and tenderness as they seek to disciple Todd in the nurture and admonition of the Lord. Father, we pray that You would bind this family close to your heart and that the roots of their lives would be planted deeply in the love of Christ.

How we pray that for Todd, that the Holy Spirit would begin even now to woo him to Christ as his Savior, that the Spirit would gently and graciously lead him to the point where he recognizes his need of Christ as his own Savior. And Father, we look forward to the day that You will lead Todd to confess with his mouth that Jesus Christ is Lord and Savior of his life. Let him be a man of God who will shoulder life's responsibilities gladly, who will graciously testify to the glory of Your name and the greatness of Your kingdom. And how we pray, Father, that You will use him to bring Your name that glory You deserve. We pray that You will lead him so clearly and definitely that there would be no question as to his allegiance or the purpose of his life. And so, Father, as a church family, we stand before You gathered here today to commit ourselves once again to this great task of making disciples, of encouraging families in this church to live godly. And how I pray that You would continue to knit our hearts together in love because of the great love You have demonstrated toward us in Your Son, Jesus. We pray all these things in Your precious name, Amen.

Smiling, I remembered how calmly Todd had lain in Pastor Danny's arms during that prayer. He was wide awake but as still as could be, dressed in the same outfit his older brother, Brandon, had worn when we dedicated him to the Lord.

My memories drifted forward eight years to Todd's baptism. Before Pastor Danny called him to the platform, Todd perched with anticipation on the edge of the pew; a smile spread across his face. I was nervous for him yet proud that he was brave enough to speak in front of our large congregation. Finally, Pastor Danny called Todd to the platform and then stood with his arm around him while Todd gave his salvation testimony. In a clear voice, he said, "My name is Todd Lurtey, and this is how I got saved and how I wanted to get saved. I was thinking about God's glory and Him shedding His blood to die on the cross for our sins. So I wanted to get saved because I knew where I was going to go—I was going to go straight down to hell. So I didn't want that; I wanted to go with the Lord up in heaven. So I got saved and I wanted to get saved because I didn't want to go down to hell. I wanted to go up into heaven with the Lord so I can spend eternal life with Him. I wanted to get baptized because it shows God's glory and that I am a Christian and I love God with my heart."

A few minutes later, as they stood in the water for the baptism, Pastor Danny prayed, "Father, thank You for your work in Todd's heart, and we pray that the joy and enthusiasm that he has shown in preparing for this public testimony and baptism would be the same joy and enthusiasm that characterizes his Christian service all the days of his life. I pray that You would grow him in godliness, in wisdom, and in the fear of the Lord. And let him be like a tree that is planted by the rivers of water, whose fruit is always being born in season, whose root never withers. And we ask, Lord God, that You would just keep your hand upon him. For it's in the name of Jesus Christ we pray, Amen."

Abruptly, I jerked back to reality. How different this day would be for my husband, David, our family, and me. I again sat in the front row, but this time Todd was not an infant in Pastor Danny's arms; he was not an eight-year-old giving his testimony on the platform; nor was he standing next to Pastor Danny in the baptismal pool. Today, Todd's precious body lay just inches in front of me at the foot of the pulpit—in a flower-draped casket.

Thoughts crowded my mind. *"How could this possibly be happening to our family? Why, Lord? We dedicated him to You. He loved You so much and wanted to serve You. We trusted You to heal him."* During Todd's illness, I pictured myself scooping up his frail body in my arms and carrying him to Jesus. Todd's situation was desperate, but I knew Jesus could heal him. I had reminded the Lord of people in the Scriptures who trusted Jesus to heal them if they could just reach Him. Matthew 8:2 says, "And behold, a leper came to him and knelt before him, saying, 'Lord, if you will, you can make me clean.' And Jesus stretched out his hand and touched him, saying, 'I will; be clean.'" Further, in the same chapter, Jesus healed a servant and a demon-possessed man. I knew God could heal Todd; the Bible proved it.

I clung desperately to the words in Matthew 9:18 when I prayed for Todd: "While he was saying these things to them, behold, a ruler came in and knelt before him, saying, 'My daughter has just died, but come and lay your hand on her, and she will live.' And Jesus rose and followed him, with his disciples. And behold a woman who had suffered from a discharge of blood for twelve years came up behind him and touched the fringe of his garment, for she said to herself, 'If I only touch his garment, I will be made well.' Jesus turned, and seeing her he said, 'Take heart, daughter, your faith has made you well.' And instantly, the woman was made well." Prayerfully, I reminded Him, *"Lord, my child is broken and I can't fix him. I know You can heal him even when nothing else has helped him and when all hope seems to be gone."* I carried Todd to the Lord with all the faith I held in my heart. I placed him in the arms of Jesus, but instead of healing Todd, He took him from me and seemingly walked away.

I questioned whether the Lord really loved me. I would never willingly hurt my child as my Heavenly Father was hurting me. My heart was breaking over Todd's death, but realizing I could no longer understand the love of God damaged me even more. My spirit went into a dark place, and I didn't know how I would recover.

Brenda Lurtey

Chapter 1

Children

My husband, David, and I welcomed our first child, Brandon David Benjamin Lurtey, into the world on July 8, 1994. I had a long and painful labor and delivery, but in the end, I held a beautiful baby boy in my arms. I fell in love with him instantly. Oddly enough, the first thing I noticed about him was his feet. Staring at them, I thought, *"Wow, he has feet!"* I have no idea what I thought would actually be attached to his legs, but his tiny feet fascinated me. Brandon had a head of blonde hair and perfect lips. I had always been a bit insecure about myself, but after delivering such an adorable baby, I felt as if I were the queen of the world. Finally, I was a mother, and I was proud of the baby the Lord gave to David and me. Although Brandon's colic dominated our early months with him, we loved him dearly. We were thankful God had placed him in our lives— crying and all.

Less than three years later, the Lord blessed us with our second child. This time, I predicted my delivery date with uncanny accuracy. Okay, I didn't really predict the day, but I prayed my baby would arrive on March 4. During my pregnancy, I worked as the receptionist in the hospital where I was scheduled to give birth. People asked me for months in advance, "When is your baby due?"

I like to joke around, so I often responded, "My baby is due on March 9, but I'm going to deliver on March 4."

The next question was inevitable. "Oh, are you having a C-section?"

"No, but my birthday is March 3, and my mother is flying in on that day, so I have decided to have the baby on March 4."

Everyone laughed as if to say "Yeah right." When coworkers questioned me about my delivery date, I confidently gave them the same answer. They responded with laughter as well. I began asking the Lord to allow me to deliver on March 4. I thought it would be funny, and it would definitely make a great story one day!

Finally, my birthday arrived. I reminded my coworkers, "By the way, I won't be in to work tomorrow."

"Why? Are you sick?"

"No, I am having my baby tomorrow, remember?"

"Are you in labor?"

"No, but today is my birthday and my mom is coming in tonight, so I will have my baby tomorrow." My coworkers insisted I would be at my desk as usual in the morning. Again I prayed and asked the Lord to let my prediction come true. Let me tell you, the Lord has a sense of humor. That night at my birthday supper, I went into labor!

As God would have it, Sharon, my college roommate, was the nurse on duty that night. We had a wonderful time as roommates and have remained close over the years. She took great care of me and graciously listened to me moan and groan all night as we walked up and down the hallway of the hospital. Even through some painful contractions, we laughed and reminisced about our college days.

The next morning my coworkers found my desk empty. They began questioning one another, "Where's Brenda?"

A nurse gave them the news. "She's up in the birthing room delivering her baby!" As my coworkers came in to visit me throughout the day, you better believe I loved saying, "See, I told you I was going to have my baby on March 4!"

At 11:50 that morning, after a fairly easy labor and a wonderful epidural, the doctor announced, "It's a boy!" as Todd Frederick James Lurtey made his entrance into the world. Having another son thrilled me, especially since Brandon now had a little playmate. Right after my delivery, for some odd reason I craved sweet tea. I almost couldn't get enough of it to drink. No wonder Todd loved sweet tea all his life!

Sharon went home to sleep for a few hours after Todd's delivery. When she came back that evening, she gave Todd his first bath before bringing him back to my room, all snuggly and clean. She swaddled him in a soft blanket and covered his head with a white hat with a baby blue pom-pom on the top. I fell in love with him as I held him close to my heart.

After two nights in the hospital, our little family of four went home to begin our lives together. Being Todd's mom was a pleasure. First of all, he was adorable, just like Brandon, but instead of blonde hair, he had a head full of thick, brown hair. From the beginning, he was a dream child. He rarely cried—even as an infant. One night, when he was just a few days old, my friend Cheryl and I chatted for quite some time while Todd lay heavy on my shoulder, breathing steadily. He was so still that I assumed he was sound asleep. I turned Todd to face Cheryl. "Is he asleep?" I whispered.

"No, actually, he's wide awake. He's just content." I adored Todd for the peaceful spirit that characterized his life as he grew older.

When he was about two weeks old, I took him to the doctor for a routine infant check up. When the nurse took off his shirt to weigh him, under the bright lights I noticed a very faint but large brown birthmark that went up the middle of his chest, around to the middle of his back, and around one arm. When the doctor came, I asked him what it was. The doctor looked at Todd more closely before telling me the mark was called a nevus. In all his years of practice, he had seen only about three cases, but he assured me we had nothing to worry about. As Todd grew, the nevus grew with him and got a bit darker, but at his regular checkups, the doctor always assured me we had no cause for alarm.

Todd was an extremely happy yet unusually quiet child. He whimpered when he was hungry and he might cry for a minute if he got hurt, but he always sobbed when I left him in the church nursery. Fortunately, his tears gave way to a huge smile when I was called back to the room to calm him down. Todd's smile was famous at our church.

As he grew, Todd shadowed Brandon anywhere and everywhere. He always wanted to do whatever Brandon was doing. They both loved playing inside with their train set, and they enjoyed playing school. Todd sat obediently in his little chair gripping his sippy cup while teacher Brandon "read" books and showed him the illustrations. Most of all, they loved romping outside, especially in their small cabin that made an awesome fort or clubhouse. Playing policemen and riding bikes were among their favorite outdoor pastimes. I can still picture Brandon pedaling his training bike, pulling Todd behind him in his little red wagon. To the boys, the bike and wagon made an exciting train. When they played police officers, Brandon would speed past Todd on his tricycle while traffic-cop Todd chased after him with his little hand held up yelling, "Stop, stop!" Every Friday, they set up their tiny beach chairs in our front yard, waiting for the garbage truck to drive through our neighborhood. The two of them treated the sanitation workers like celebrities, waving enthusiastically at them as they drove down our street.

The Lord gave Brandon and Todd a special bond. They played happily together, shared a room decorated with trains, and loved each other dearly. They were best friends. I expected their connection to last long after David and I were gone.

By age three, I noticed Todd always positioned himself close to whatever he wanted to see. I suspected he needed glasses, and I was correct. He had bad eyesight for a three-year-old. When we got home from the eye doctor, he peered up at the trees through his new glasses, smiled, and said, "Mommy, I see leaves!"

I almost cried thinking how much he had missed in his first few years of life. No wonder he was quiet; he couldn't see anything to talk about! I am slightly biased, but I thought Todd looked adorable with his glasses and perpetual smile. Todd was rough on his glasses; we took them in for repair constantly. He even broke them twice in one afternoon. The workers at the optical store shook their heads and grinned as Todd, with very bent glasses perched on his beaming face, strolled happily back into the store. In no time, they all knew him by name. No matter what was going on around him, the joy that characterized his life was contagious!

Three years after Todd's birth, it was time for the Lurteys to think pink. I delivered our daughter, Lauren Mary Nicole Lurtey, on June 4, 2000. We were thrilled to have a little girl in the family. At first Brandon didn't understand what my pregnancy meant. As we rode bikes together at the beach, I thought it was the perfect time to tell him we were expecting a new baby. Casually, I asked, "Brandon, would you like to have a new brother or sister?"

He furrowed his brow, thought long and hard, and then replied, "No, I think I will just keep Todd."

Laughing, I assured him we would keep Todd no matter what, but then I added, "Well, we are going to have another baby."

His reaction was not what I expected; he was very disappointed. "Aw, Mom, does Daddy know about this?"

"Uh, yes, Brandon. Daddy definitely knows about it!"

A few months later, Lauren came into the world with a full set of lungs. I could not believe that after two rowdy boys, I finally had a little girl. All I knew as a mom up to that point was boys and their toys. I loved playing with dolls when I was little, and now I had my own baby girl to dress up. I could not wait to buy hair bows, tiny black shoes, and little white tights for her! In no time, Brandon and Todd adored their new baby sister. Her first Christmas, she played the part of "baby Jesus" in Brandon and Todd's annual family Christmas play. It was the first time I had ever seen baby Jesus played by a little blonde girl with pink sponge curlers in her hair. I was content. My family—two boys and one girl—was complete . . . or so I thought.

"Lord, what? I'm pregnant? I just lost all my baby weight from the last three! We can't afford it. We don't have a big enough house. We were all done having children. It's not in my plan!" Ready or not, here he comes. On April 12, 2003, almost three years after Lauren's birth, Jeffrey Joseph Mark Lurtey entered the world. Although he was our surprise baby, he truly was a welcome addition to the family. We were grateful the Lord gave us what we did not necessarily ask for but what He knew we needed for our family to be complete.

Lauren now took on the role of big sister. She loved pushing Jeffrey around in her doll stroller; he was her real, live, baby doll. Todd adored Jeffrey and immediately stepped into the role of protective big brother. Most pictures of Todd and Jeffrey show Todd's arms draped over Jeffrey's shoulders or wrapped securely around his back.

Each of our children has a unique personality. Brandon cried a lot as a baby and chattered almost incessantly as a child, but he grew into a loving and sweet young man. Todd was happy and compliant with anything that went on around him. Lauren was sometimes slightly emotional and not altogether thrilled that she had only brothers in her life, but she enjoyed mothering Jeffrey and usually played contentedly with her dolls by herself.

And Jeffrey? Few who meet Jeffrey soon forget him. His behavior at daycare, the church nursery, and our home made him a near legend. He is an accomplished escape artist whose skills have our church nursery workers talking about him to this day. When Jeffrey was two, I asked Brandon, Todd, and Lauren to take care of him while I dried my hair. Their eyes were glued to cartoons in the family room, but they agreed, with glazed-over stares and groans, to keep an eye on him. I had almost finished drying my hair when a sick sense came over me—call it "mother's intuition." I thought, *"Hmmmmmm . . ."* A moment later the front doorbell rang. A stranger stood on the porch, holding Jeffrey, dressed only in a diaper, by the hand. Shocked, I asked, "Oh, my goodness! Where was he?"

The man pointed to a construction site across the street. "Over there."

Defensively, I explained I had no idea Jeffrey was even out of the house. "All the doors were locked, and his brothers and sister were supposed to be watching him."

The man was unmoved by my excuse. "Lady, he's been over there twice!"

Not long after that incident, once again, as I dried my hair, that now familiar uneasy feeling came over me. I turned off the hair dryer and started looking for Jeffrey. I found the kitchen full of smoke. Through the haze, I spotted Jeffrey, who had somehow figured out how to turn the microwave on, sitting on the counter, nuking the plastic box of donuts I kept stored inside. I made a mental note to myself: plastic is not microwaveable, and don't blow-dry your hair anymore!

One Wednesday night, when Jeffrey was four, our church hosted a blood drive. I asked Todd to watch Jeffrey while I donated. "No problem," he assured me. After I finished, I walked down the hallway searching for Todd and Jeffrey. A few moments later, I spotted Todd walking alone toward me.

"Where's Jeffrey?"

Todd shrugged his shoulders. "I don't know. He ran away from me."

I wondered why Todd didn't try to catch him, but I could not waste time finding out the answer. I was not terribly nervous since we were in our church, but I definitely wanted to find Jeffrey before he found trouble. Seconds later, a church member walked toward me holding Jeffrey's hand.

Curious, I asked, "Where did you find him?"

"He was climbing out of the baptistery." I thank the Lord it was empty at the time!

Of all my dreams and plans for my children, I cared most that each one of them would desire a relationship with Jesus and would one day accept His free gift of salvation and ask Him to be their Savior. I took every opportunity to talk with them about the Lord. One afternoon as Todd and I sat at the kitchen table, I took the opportunity to explain how he could know he would go to heaven one day. As I spoke, he looked in my eyes, listening intently. I told him he was born a sinner, as we all are, but that Jesus loved him so much He died on the cross for Todd's sins and for the sins of the world. He took the punishment we deserved, and in return He gave us a free gift. I told Todd that if he asked Jesus to forgive him for his sins, Jesus would come into his heart and give him the gift of eternal life in heaven. After I laid out the gospel as clearly as I could, I asked with a hopeful heart, "Todd, would you like to ask Jesus to come into your heart?"

His focused look shifted to one of shock. Laughing nervously, he yelled out, "No way! Is He going to go down my throat?"

Obviously, Todd was not quite ready for salvation. About a year or so later, he finally understood what having Jesus in his heart means, and he accepted Jesus as his Savior. From that time on, Todd loved Jesus and wanted to tell everyone about Him. Eventually all four of our children gave their hearts to Jesus.

Our kids all loved each other, and they each had a partner—Brandon with Todd and Lauren with Jeffrey. We moved into a bigger house, and after Jeffrey was born, he and Todd shared a room. As a result, they grew very close despite their age difference.

God blessed David and me with each of our precious children, but I always wondered why the Lord chose to give us four. I wasn't complaining; I was thankful. It was just something I often wondered about. Every time I saw a picture of my children together, I counted them: one . . . two . . . three . . . four. When we went anywhere together, I often counted them to make sure they were still all there. I cherished each of them, and on many occasions I had the strange thought, *"I hope I always have four children."* It seemed odd to me that I felt the need to count them as often as I did, but as I look back over what has transpired in our family, I now believe the Lord was preparing me for a day when my children would no longer be all together on this earth. It was a powerful intuition I tried desperately to dismiss.

Chapter 2

Neurofibromatosis

Todd was my random child. He often did or said funny things unexpectedly. Mornings were hectic at our house as we scrambled around getting breakfast, packing lunches, and making certain the kids all had their books together. One morning, as I quizzed them on whether they had eaten and brushed their teeth, Todd kept interrupting me. "Mom!"

I responded, "Just a minute, Todd," before continuing my questions and instructions. I barely got another sentence out before Todd interrupted again. "Mom!"

"Just a minute, Todd."

This exchange went on for a few moments. Finally I stopped and gave him my full attention. "Yes, Todd. What is it?"

He said, very seriously, "When you get old, I'll spoon-feed you your jello!"

I looked at him in amazement, thinking, *"Really, Todd? That's what was so important?"* I thanked him, shook my head at the randomness of his comment, and continued with my preparations for the day.

One of my sister Corinne's all-time favorite "random Todd comments" took place at our family dinner table. All four kids had spent the entire day bickering. Eventually, I lost my cool with them and demanded they stop all the fighting and learn to get along. "I'm sick and tired of all the bickering!" I muttered.

That evening at supper, David asked Todd whether he would like to pray before the meal. Todd thanked the Lord for the food, added a few more remarks, and then closed his prayer, "And dear Lord, please help Mommy to feel better . . ." I lifted my head and looked at David just as he lifted his head and looked at me. Confused, I thought, *"I'm not sick. I feel fine,"* just as Todd continued, "... because she is sick and tired of all the bickering going on in this house!" David and I burst out laughing, as a truer word had never been spoken!

I love to have fun with my kids, so around the Lurtey household, the magic word was not always "please." Sometimes, when my kids wanted a special treat or favor, the magic word they knew they needed to add was really a magic sentence: "Mom, may I have a cookie . . . and by the way, you look like you've lost weight." They knew they could usually get what they wanted with that compliment! Perhaps I was a bit sensitive about my weight, and their tongue-in-cheek comment took some of the sting out of reality. I could count on Todd to bring it back, though. One night at supper I told the kids that Prince Edward was visiting our town and that I had actually seen him. Todd responded, "Wow, did you get to talk to him?"

I answered, "Oh, no. You have to be a 'bigwig' in order to actually talk to him."

In all seriousness, and without a bit of malice, Todd replied, "Well, you're big." Oh, yes, he did!

Brandon, always my protector, smiled and asked, "Mom, can I?"

With a huge grin, I answered, "Absolutely." With that, Brandon pulled Todd to the ground and playfully beat the tar out of him—with my blessing!

Of all the random comments Todd made in his lifetime, one sticks out the most in my mind. He walked into the dining room and said very calmly, "Mom, I might die when I'm young."

Shocked, I said, "Todd, don't say that! I don't want you to die when you are young!"

Nonchalantly, he replied, "Well, if God wants me, He wants me, and there is nothing you can do about it." With that, he turned and walked out of the room. My heart grabbed with fear, but I tried to dismiss his words as childish thoughts. Unfortunately, I later had good reason to remember them.

When Todd was about seven years old, as I washed his arms during a bath, I noticed a marble-sized lump in the arm that had the nevus. Instantly I worried it might be a cancerous tumor. The next day I took him to the doctor to have the lump examined. The doctor told me he thought it had always been there, but I knew this was not the case. Because of my fear, he referred us to a general surgeon, who ordered a biopsy after examining Todd. Unfortunately, we couldn't get an immediate appointment for the biopsy, so we had to wait a few agonizing days.

We had a family trip scheduled during that time and decided to go ahead with our plans. One evening, as David and I sat talking on the hotel balcony overlooking a small river, Todd came out and settled on my lap. I wrapped my arms around him and began sobbing silently, something I later became very good at. Todd, oblivious to my tears, chatted away with his father, while I held on to him for dear life. Tears streamed steadily down my cheeks as I prayerfully begged, *"God, please don't take my precious little boy away from me."* As I pleaded with God, Satan reminded me of all the terrible things that could happen to Todd. One sentence seemed to be constant.

"You can plan Todd's funeral because he is going to die."

Even after we came home from our trip, Satan continued tormenting me.

In the days leading up to the biopsy, I tucked Todd into bed each night. Though he happily turned over to fall asleep, I left his room in tears, wondering if he were going to die. I was borrowing trouble from tomorrow when we still had no idea what we were facing.

Todd went in for his biopsy with little to no fear. He had already had two non-related surgical procedures in his lifetime, so he was no stranger to the operating room. When the surgeon met David and me after the biopsy, he said, "Well, it was what I thought it was. It's just a fibroma." I had never heard the word "fibroma" before, but I knew it was not cancer. Relief flooded me. The surgeon referred Todd to a specialist in Wake Forest, North Carolina. During that appointment, after the doctor checked Todd over, he diagnosed him with neurofibromatosis. My first thought was *"Neuro-what?"*

The doctor said, "Does anyone in your family have neurofibromatosis?"

Confidently, I replied, "No, I have never even heard of that word. What is it?" He told me some of the symptoms—small squishy tumors, freckling under the armpits and in the groin area, and five or more café au lait spots on the body.

"I don't know what café au lait spots are, but I have some birthmarks and this chicken pox scar." I showed him the markings.

After he checked my markings he said, "You're the carrier. You have neurofibromatosis."

He told me neurofibromatosis is a disease that causes tumors to grow. He was quick to inform me that most of the time these tumors are benign, and I was relieved. I was not upset about hearing the diagnosis. I actually found it interesting, but I wondered why in all of my lifetime of doctor visits, no doctor had ever diagnosed me with this disease. As we discussed the symptoms, I told the specialist that if Todd and I had neurofibromatosis, then I was sure Brandon and Lauren had the disease as well. I knew they each had the axillary freckling and five or more café au lait spots that the doctor pointed out on Todd's body and on mine. The specialist recommended that we visit a geneticist in our hometown and released us from his care.

With this trial seemingly behind us, I did some research about our new diagnosis. I was amazed, as the research affirmed what the specialist had told me, that the markings on my body I had always thought were just birthmarks, the café au lait spots, were actually characteristics of the disease. The bump on my arm I always thought was a chicken pox scar was really a soft tumor called a neurofibroma. My NF1 symptoms had obviously never bothered me since up to this point I never even knew I had the disease. I also found out that in addition to the skin issues my children and I had, there were other potential complications with NF1. Lisch nodules, or tiny bumps on the iris of the eye, can form. Bone deformities, such as scoliosis, are common in NF1 patients—Brandon, Todd, and Lauren had all previously been diagnosed with scoliosis. I read that children with NF1 often have specific learning disabilities— Brandon, Todd, and Lauren all struggled with learning disabilities. It was no surprise to me when a geneticist later determined I was right—both Brandon and Lauren also had neurofibromatosis. I learned my disease was not genetic; it was the result of a spontaneous gene mutation. As a carrier, I had a 50/50 chance of passing the disease along to each of my children. By the time I found out about the disease, I had four children and had unknowingly given it to Brandon, Todd, and Lauren, but not Jeffrey. Looking back, I am grateful the Lord did not reveal my disease to me until all four of them were born. Had I known I had neurofibromatosis before having children, I may have been tempted to live in fear throughout my pregnancies. Thankfully, I read that only 7% of all fibromas ever turn cancerous. That was great news. I thought we would not have any cause for further concern.

Honestly, the freckling and café au lait spots were somewhat embarrassing—now that I knew we had this disease. Brandon, Lauren, Todd, and I were all asked at different times why our skin had so many spots. We gave inquirers a brief description of our genetic disease. The kids were still quite young at this time, and they did not allow comments to affect them. On several occasions, young children asked Todd, with looks of disgust, "What is that thing on your arm [referring to the nevus]?" Todd confidently replied, "It's just a birthmark" and he rarely seemed to be affected by the comments.

Occasionally I saw the looks of disgust and my feelings were hurt. I often read and tried to claim Psalm 139:14, "I praise you, for I am fearfully and wonderfully made," and Psalm 139:16, "Your eyes saw my unformed substance." God saw how we were being formed, and we were perfect in His sight. Believing God made my children perfectly in His image was easier than thinking that about myself. I wanted the perfect skin I perceived other people had, but I knew I needed to view myself through God's eyes and stop thinking He had somehow made a mistake with the way He made me.

Brenda Lurtey

Chapter 3

I Hear Music

Brandon has many of the physical traits of NF1, but they never adversely affected his overall health. Lauren, however, was born with a sunken chest. At the time I delivered her, David and I thought the sunken chest was solely a birth defect. Now we believe that her bone deformity may be part of the NF1 disease. On Mother's Day, May 10, 2009, I gave a testimony via video in our church about God's hand on Lauren during a particularly difficult time in her life.

When my daughter, Lauren, was an infant, we noticed that her sternum did not look exactly right. The doctor later confirmed that she had pectus excavatum, an abnormal growth of the rib cage that causes the sternum to be sunken. Since she was so young, there was nothing that could be done to correct it until she was older. At age three, our primary care doctor felt it was time for Lauren to see a pediatric surgeon, because the sternum seemed to be getting worse. The surgeon told me that she would eventually need surgery, but since she was still too young, he would just continue to monitor her. Just two years later, he realized that the surgery to fix her chest could not wait. Her sternum was almost touching her spine and her heart was being pushed out of the way. A few days after Lauren turned five, she had a surgery called the Nuss Procedure to fix her sternum. The surgeon made an incision under Lauren's arms, inserted a pectus bar under her sternum concave, and then flipped the bar over. It popped the sternum out. The surgery was rough, and the recovery was extremely painful for Lauren. The bar did bring out the sternum some and allowed her heart to move back into the proper position; however, the surgery was not completely successful. The surgeon noticed right away that the cartilage at the end of each of her ribs buckled. I noticed that as well. We did not learn until many years later that Lauren's collarbone was dislocated at the time.

Later we noticed that her face seemed to be growing asymmetrically, and her permanent teeth were growing in far out of alignment. I took Lauren to a dentist, who noticed a lot of problems and referred her to an orthodontist. He, through the doctor, requested that Lauren go for a CT scan.

When the results were ready, I picked up the CT scan report and took a copy to the doctor's office. Early the next morning, the doctor called me and told me that the CT scan had revealed a mass at the base of her skull. I asked him if he was concerned. He said, "Yes, I am." He told me he was ordering an MRI to get a clearer image of the mass. The verse that meant a lot to me during the waiting period was Psalm 139:16: "Your eyes saw my unformed substance." I read those first three words over and over again—"Your eyes saw." It's funny that I have read this particular verse many times in past years, but at this point, I really noticed it. It meant something to me. God saw everything about the way Lauren was being formed before her birth, and the rest of our family, for that matter. He is the one who formed her just like she is. He knows all and sees all. He sees the mass. He knows exactly what it is. Even though our NF1 disease baffles some doctors, God knows all about it and its complications are no surprise to Him.

The Lord also brought to mind the fact that David and I had publicly dedicated each of our children to the Lord. The Lord, in a still, small voice, spoke to my heart and said, *"Did you mean it?"* I wondered whether I really had given my children to Him with my whole heart. That was hard to answer. I really wanted to mean it, but there was a lot at stake. To me, their dedication meant I had to be willing to let God do whatever He wanted to do with their lives—allow them to suffer without being bitter, even allow God to take their lives if He chose to do that—without being bitter. I know God understands the love of a mother and how hard this was for me. Again, Psalm 139 speaks of this. "O Lord, you have searched me and known me" (v. 1). He knows me like no one else does. I wanted to have the right spirit no matter what the results of Lauren's MRI would be, but it was just so hard to actually have the right spirit and mean it. God knew the deepest thoughts in my heart—there was no fooling Him.

On the day of the MRI, I had given Lauren some medication from the doctor to help calm her a bit. As we were driving to the hospital, Lauren was quietly playing in the back seat, and I was trying desperately not to cry. I began to very quietly sing the song that the church choir had just sung a few days earlier, "Be Not Afraid."

Lauren had big crocodile tears in her eyes as we waited right outside the MRI room. I was trying hard to be brave and not cry myself, but it was hard to see her so fearful. I reminded her that God would be with her and that there were a lot of people praying for her. I hugged her and we prayed together and then it was time to go into the MRI room.

It was hard seeing the radiologist strap her on the table and place the head shield on her. It was even harder watching her little body enter that machine, knowing why she was going in there and knowing how afraid she was. I really broke down after she entered the machine—I didn't feel like being brave anymore. Within a minute or two, the Lord drew my attention to her feet and I noticed how still she was lying. I didn't see her toes move a muscle—not even once. I thought she had fallen asleep, and that made me feel at ease. I began to pray for Lauren, and I felt what I could only describe as a blanket of peace come over me. It was cold in the room and I was shivering, but in that moment, it felt like someone had literally placed a warm blanket on my back and around my shoulders, and I knew people were praying on Laurean's behalf. I, too, kept praying over and over that Lauren would sense that the Lord was right beside her.

After about twenty-five minutes, the radiologist came in and pulled the table out of the machine to administer some contrast in her IV before the last part of the MRI. To my great surprise, Lauren was awake and had not been asleep at all. God had kept her perfectly still just like I prayed. I was AMAZED!

When the last portion of the MRI was finished, the radiologist came in and told us that they had gotten clear pictures and we could leave. All we could do now was wait for the results.

At supper that evening as different ones were talking, Lauren quietly said to me out of the blue, "Mommy, when I was in that machine, I felt like God had His arms wrapped around me really tight." At first I was shocked, and then I thought, "Oh, that must have just been the . . ." and my thoughts quickly trailed off. In the instant of that sinful thought, the Lord spoke to my heart with the loudest, inaudible words that I have ever heard, *"HOW DARE YOU TRY TO REASON THIS AWAY!"* I was startled and realized what an ungodly thought had entered my head. Of course He could be with her in an MRI machine! Why wouldn't He be with His child when she needed Him and when so many people had specifically asked Him to be with her? I felt very ashamed and rebuked.

I then asked Lauren to demonstrate what God's arms felt like. She came up behind me and wrapped her arms very tightly around me. I realized what an answer to prayer God had really given me. The whole time that Lauren was in the MRI machine, I kept praying that she would know God's presence—that she would know He was right beside her—but He was doing better than that. He was holding her.

After I had put Lauren to bed that night, she got back up and said she wasn't feeling well and asked to sit with me for a while. We started talking about the procedure again, and I said, "Lauren, was it very loud in that machine?" I asked her that because I had earplugs in and the sound from the machine was still loud to me.

She looked at me a little surprised and said, "Not really; I heard music."

Surprised, I said, "You heard music?"

She said, "Yes, didn't you?"

I said, "No, I didn't; what did you hear?"

She said, "You know that song 'Be Not Afraid'? I heard that song." I instantly felt chilled and thought that must have been an amazing experience for her. This time, I had no intention of questioning her statement! I knew the Lord had placed that music in the MRI machine to comfort His scared little girl. I knew no music from the hospital was being piped into the room. I told her that was a precious gift from God to her because I didn't hear the music. She just shrugged her shoulders and said, "Well, I did."

It was days later that I realized that God had given us comfort in the exact same song, but for each of us, it was at the time when we needed it most. A few days later, Lauren said, "Mom, when I was in the MRI machine, it felt like God was rocking me. Not back and forth like I was on a swing, but like I was in a cradle."

I cannot imagine what Lauren experienced in the MRI machine, but to me, it must have been something divine, and I will always be thankful for what the Lord did for her.

The results of the MRI were termed "uneventful." I thought it was all plenty eventful. The doctors believe that the mass is just a fibroma.

God is teaching me that it is important not to hold on to my children too tightly. They really belong to God, and He just allows me the privilege of taking care of them for His glory. That's a really sobering thought because I feel like they are MINE. But, truly, they are HIS. I cannot control what He wants to do in their lives. I have to entrust my children to Him, knowing that He has their best interests at heart—even if He would choose to let them suffer or even take their life. Humanly speaking, it is very hard to entrust my children to the Lord, yet He loves my children more than I love them. I am also learning that when we ask God for the desires of our heart, we should wait expectantly for Him to answer our requests. Why are we so surprised when He actually answers our requests?

We have no way of knowing what the future holds for our family in regard to this disease (NF1), but God has it all planned out. We can choose to live in fear, or we can choose to trust our future to Him. I think one reason that the Lord has allowed us to experience what we did with Todd and then with Lauren is to show us His faithfulness. If, and when, a new trial comes up for our family, we can look to these past experiences and remember how the Lord was present with our family during our time of need and that He faithfully carried us through these times. As He has been with us in the past, so will He be with us in the future. It is my prayer that God will give each of us the grace and strength we need to trust Him with our future and not be afraid.

> Be not afraid, for I have redeemed you.
> Be not afraid, I have called you by name.
> When you pass through the waters, I will be with you.
> When you pass through floods, they will not sweep o'er you.
> When you walk through the fire, you will not be consumed.
> You are mine, you are precious in my sight. (Courtney)

I sat in the service with Todd by my side the day the video was presented to our church. Little did I know that exactly four years later, the Lord would put my very words to the ultimate test.

Brenda Lurtey

Chapter 4

Pain and Fear

Todd loved life and his smile was infectious. I think it is safe to say that everyone who knew him well would agree with me. He loved people and wanted to participate in every activity involving friends at church and at school. He enjoyed young children and often volunteered in the church nursery. He loved to help with dishes in the church kitchen after a church-wide supper or to help neighbors do yard work. What may surprise some people is that he even enjoyed being with his parents' friends. He grew up in our church, so he had known our friends his entire life and felt free to joke around with them. He loved all kinds of sports—basketball, baseball, and soccer, but especially swimming. Not a summer went by that he, Brandon, Lauren, and Jeffrey did not spend the majority of the day in the water.

With all the joy that characterized Todd's life, I grew concerned when in August 2012 I noticed a darkness that had crept into Todd's spirit. His familiar smile faded. He seemed irritable, even angry at times, and just was not acting like his normal, sweet self. One night I told David we really needed to pray for Todd; it seemed as if we were in a battle for his soul.

Later that month, David took Todd to the doctor for his fall sports physical. He was always a slim child, so his fifteen-pound weight loss caused us some concern. At the time, since Todd had no other physical ailments that would cause any alarm, the doctor just told Todd to make sure he ate a good breakfast every day and to try to gain some weight. Otherwise, he pronounced Todd in good physical health. He certainly acted healthy; he had even won the Presidential Physical Fitness Award on May 10, 2012.

You know how life can change in just a moment? My comfortable world forever changed with one statement: "Mom, my side hurts."

Todd was a few weeks into his first year of high school when our extended family, eighteen people in all, left for a trip to Disney World. My brother, Brent, and his family, missionaries in South Africa, were home on furlough. All six cousins, my brother and sister and their spouses, my parents, and David and I and our children were having one last hurrah before my brother and his family returned to South Africa for their next mission term. We packed every day with excitement, attending shows, riding the attractions, eating like kings and queens, and making precious memories. Everything seemed perfect until Todd came into my room one evening and said, "Mom, my side hurts." My heart instantly grabbed, but I brushed aside my fears.

Handing him some Tylenol, I reassured him. "Maybe you got banged up on a ride, Todd." Inside, though, I wondered if something really might be seriously wrong. Over the next few days, Todd continued to join in the fun, but we noticed him hold his side from time to time.

When we got home from the trip, the pain still bothered him, so I took him to our family doctor. Dr. Harding could not feel anything protruding from his side, and no amount of pushing made Todd wince, so he scheduled an MRI for October 12 to see whether anything was going on internally.

Late afternoon on October 12, Dr. Harding called and asked David and me to come to his office immediately because he saw something on the MRI that concerned him. At the meeting, he advised us that the MRI showed a large mass, and we needed to see a pediatric surgeon right away. The appointment was scheduled quickly, which was good but scary at the same time. In my experience, quick appointments highlight the seriousness of the situation.

David, Todd, and I met with the pediatric surgeon, Dr. John, on Monday afternoon. He had reviewed the MRI but told us the mass was so large he could not even see the whole thing. He wanted a clearer picture, so he ordered a CT scan. He also wanted Todd to have some blood work done. He assured us he would be in touch within the next few days. While we waited, Todd tried to attend school, but sometimes the pain was too much to bear, so he would call me and ask to come home. Todd never appeared worried. Although he was obviously hurting, he was peaceful.

On Friday afternoon, Dr. John called to deliver the results of the CT scan. There was definitely a very large tumor in Todd's abdomen, one that would require a biopsy. The biopsy was scheduled for October 24, 2012. With an unsteady voice, I asked, "Do you think the tumor is malignant?"

He responded quietly, "Yes, I do."

I tried to be brave while we discussed the upcoming biopsy details, but when I hung up the phone, the tears began to flow. Kneeling down by my bed, I sobbed one phrase over and over again: "God, please don't take my baby; please don't take my baby." Grief overwhelmed me. I did not know what else to say to the Lord. I cried off and on for the rest of that day and mostly stayed in my room to hide my tears from the kids, especially Todd. I was not ready to let him know my fears. The Lord was so kind to send dear friends to our aid that evening. Barry and Carol had a cancer scare with their daughter Christine when she was an infant, and they knew the fear we were facing. I was thankful they took the time to call and talk to David and me and to encourage us not to lose heart—especially when we were not even certain Todd had cancer. Although my tears still flowed, their words and assurances of prayer helped to remind us that we were not alone.

By late Saturday afternoon I still could not stop crying, and I knew I needed help to get through what might lie ahead. David arranged for us to meet with Pastor Danny and his wife, Kristen. I sobbed as we walked into the church, but their hugs and words of compassion calmed me. I wanted Pastor Danny to tell us everything would turn out fine, but he never said those words, and my heart felt unsettled. He prayed with us and reminded us to dwell on what we knew to be true at the time. What we knew to be true was that we would not know for sure whether the tumor was malignant until after the biopsy. We had to fully commit the situation to the Lord. I left the church feeling much more at peace with whatever lay ahead for Todd and our family. On Sunday, our friend Glenn held a special time of prayer for David and me, and especially for Todd, asking that God's will would be accomplished in everything.

After church, Pastor Danny asked whether David and I would like the elders to lay hands on Todd and pray for him that evening. We definitely wanted that to happen. Next, he asked whether we wanted them to anoint Todd with oil. I was familiar with the passages of Scripture detailing the anointing of oil in the Bible, but I wasn't sure what it meant or why we should do it now. Danny explained that anointing a person with oil is symbolic, just as communion is symbolic. The oil isn't a magic potion; it represents healing, just as communion represents the death, burial, and resurrection of Christ. After hearing this explanation, David and I agreed we wanted Todd to take part in the symbolism.

That evening, a group of godly men met with our family in the pastor's office after the service. Todd sat in a chair with the men surrounding him. Jeffrey sat protectively at his feet. They placed their hands on his shoulders and each man prayed that the mass would not be cancerous, but if it were, that God would grant complete healing. They also prayed for comfort and strength for Todd and our family. After the prayer time, it was so precious to see each man wrap Todd in his arms. My boy was dearly loved.

This time of prayer filled us with hope and gave us great strength for the days ahead.

Chapter 5

Diagnosis

As we drove to the hospital on October 24, I wondered what the day held for us. We had prepared all that we could, and we knew many friends and family members were praying for Todd. I wasn't overcome with fear, but I was apprehensive. Todd didn't seem nervous, but physically, he was miserable. His side hurt, but more than that, because he had to fast before the procedure, he was starving. After the nurse prepped Todd, an emergency took his spot in the operating room, so his surgery was delayed. This only added to his misery. I felt terrible for him; I wanted him to sleep so he wouldn't feel hunger or pain for a while.

While we waited for the procedure to begin, Pastor Danny walked into the room. He has always been such a comfort in our lives and always came to pray with us before various medical procedures—including Lauren's chest surgery. His presence at the hospital was perfectly normal, but we never took it for granted. He could have just prayed from home, but instead, he got ready early in the morning and drove in to be with us. He sat on Todd's bed, took Todd's hand in his own and began to pray. As I listened to Pastor Danny's words to the Lord, spoken on Todd's behalf, I felt privileged to be part of such an intimate conversation.

When the surgeon was finally ready for Todd, we walked with him right to the operating room door. I gave Todd a kiss and tried to walk away before he saw my tears. Dr. John planned to biopsy the tumor, and, if possible, remove it. I almost told him, "Just wait until you get in there. You are going to see a miracle." Although I remained silent, I had confidence in the Lord's power to heal.

First, I wondered whether the Lord had miraculously removed the tumor after the elders prayed for Todd. Perhaps Dr. John wouldn't find anything when he opened Todd up. If he did find the tumor, I was confident he would be able to remove the whole thing, it would be benign, and we could get on with our lives. This, at least, was my plan.

A nurse escorted us to a waiting room where several close friends greeted us. We had a long wait ahead, and our friends were careful not to talk too much—they just wanted to be with us. Before we went to the hospital, I hadn't wanted anyone to sit with us; I just wanted to be alone to pray and think. As always, the Lord knew what we needed more than we did—we needed to know we were not alone and that people cared about our family. As I looked around at the concerned faces of our friends, I knew they were silently praying that the surgeon would successfully remove the entire tumor.

Our friends offered to get David and me food and coffee from time to time. I hadn't eaten breakfast because I was too nervous, and I didn't want Todd to feel worse if he saw me eat. I decided to wait and enjoy food with Todd. The hospital assigned Todd's case a number that appeared on a monitor, allowing us to see where the surgeon was in the procedure. The monitor would show us when the surgery started, when it was in full swing, and when Todd was in recovery. My eyes stayed glued to his number. I actually wanted the surgery to take a long time. I knew if Dr. John came out quickly, the news would not be good—it would mean he could not get it all.

The more time went by, the more I thought Dr. John would have a good report. I kept praying for a miracle and tried to have faith that God would do the seemingly impossible. Shortly after the two-hour mark, Dr. John came out and called David and me into a nearby private room. He assured us that the procedure had gone well and informed us that the nurses were cleaning Todd up before moving him to recovery. I eagerly asked, "Did you get out the whole tumor?"

His response was not what I wanted—or expected—to hear.

"Oh, no, it took me two hours just to get a safe sample of the tumor."

He again told us he thought it would turn out to be malignant. Disappointment flooded me. In my plan, Dr. John was supposed to be shocked when he opened Todd up and saw there really was no tumor. Instead, he found just what he expected to find. To make matters worse, he not only saw the mass, but he also could not remove it, dashing my other expectation. I was not angry with God, just troubled that He hadn't answered my prayers. I wanted more out of Him. I had no idea what He was doing.

As David and I walked back into the waiting area, our friends' eyes searched ours to see what kind of news we had received. With sadness, we reported that Dr. John had not been able to remove the tumor and that he thought it was malignant. Our friends followed us into a private room where several of them took turns praying for our family. Many of them cried, yet while they were crying, I felt peace in the midst of heartache. It isn't that I wasn't sad or disappointed; I just felt the Lord's strength and presence.

I couldn't wait to see Todd and be with him again. After what seemed like a long wait, the nurses moved him from the recovery room and settled him in a regular room on the sixth floor of the hospital. He had a very long biopsy incision, but otherwise he was doing well. Still, I was almost afraid to touch him. Thankfully, he had to remain in the hospital for a few days, where the nurses could care for him. I planned to stay by his side until he could leave the hospital with me.

On Friday, as Todd sat quietly in a chair and I stared out the window, I heard a noise behind me. I turned to find Dr. John and another doctor standing in our room. Before I knew what hit me, Dr. John delivered the news I didn't want to hear. The tumor was exactly what he thought it would be—a malignant peripheral nerve sheath tumor.

My heart was calm before Dr. John entered the room, and though he said the words no one ever wants to hear, it did not skip a beat. His news didn't fill me with fear; I didn't gasp. All I felt was peace. I looked at Todd and asked, "Are you ok?"

He said, steadily, "Yes."

To my surprise, he looked up at Dr. John and asked, "So, this is a good thing, right?"

"What a strange question for him to ask. What made him ask that question?" I wondered.

"Yes, actually it is a good thing." Dr. John explained that they hoped to shrink the tumor with chemo and safely remove it. The tumor would not have responded to chemo if it was not malignant, and it was too large to remove safely at its current size.

Before he left, Dr. John very kindly asked, "Todd, is there anything we can do for you?"

Todd responded, matter-of-factly, "Yes, can you guys help me get back in the bed?"

His question struck me as hilarious and, in true Todd form, random. Of all the questions a kid who just received a cancer diagnosis could ask, he settled on that one. I would have asked whether the cancer was serious or whether I was going to die—anything but this. Under different circumstances, I would have told Todd we should call his nurse; doctors didn't do that kind of thing. Instead, I thought, *"These guys just delivered this poor kid quite a blow, so I am going to let them help him."*

Watching two important surgeons struggle to get a patient—wires and all—back into bed was funny. Laughing, Dr. John told Todd the nurses were the ones trained to help patients with this kind of task. I was just grateful they were willing to help him themselves.

When we were alone, I asked again, "Todd, are you really okay?"

He answered in an even voice, "Yes, Mom, I am." I could tell he meant it. Even after Dr. John and his colleague left, Todd never asked why he had cancer or whether I thought he was going to die. Neither of us cried. Both of us were calm. I thought, *"Wow, it really is true. God's peace is there when you need it."* I think that was the first time I had experienced that kind of complete and perfect peace. I cried when I worried about whether Todd had cancer as a young child and even before the current diagnosis, and I cried when I worried about whether Lauren had cancer; but when I had the truth—it was truly cancer—God fulfilled his promise, and it was amazing. Philippians 4:6–7 says, "Do not be anxious about anything, but in everything by prayer and supplication with thanksgiving let your requests be made known to God. And the peace of God, which surpasses all understanding, will guard your hearts and your minds in Christ Jesus." I could not understand His peace, but it overwhelmed me.

I had never heard the name of Todd's tumor before that day, so after he fell asleep that night, I did a google search to obtain some information. I read that, according to the Mayo Clinic,

> Malignant peripheral nerve sheath tumors are a type of cancer that occurs in the protective lining of the nerves that extend from the spinal cord into the body. . . .

> Malignant peripheral nerve sheath tumors can occur anywhere in the body, but most often occur in the deep tissue of the arms, legs and trunk. Malignant peripheral nerve sheath tumors tend to cause pain and weakness in the affected area and may also cause a growing lump or mass.

> Malignant peripheral nerve sheath tumors occur more frequently in people with an inherited condition that causes nerve tumors (neurofibromatosis) and in people who have undergone radiation therapy for cancer.
> (Mayo Foundation, "Definition")

I was sad that Todd was part of the 7% of people whose neurofibromatosis tumors turned cancerous.

Within a day or so of Todd's cancer diagnosis, we met with an oncologist, Dr. Alan, and Amy, a children's social worker. Dr. Alan explained the chemotherapy medications he would use for Todd's treatment and what they should accomplish. Having a plan in place for Todd gave me comfort and hope. Dr. Alan and Amy were both so kind and compassionate, and I immediately felt comfortable with them. Everything seemed under control, and I trusted that after several treatments Todd would be okay. He needed another surgery on Monday to have his port placed for chemotherapy, and then we would move to the fifth-floor children's cancer wing.

Sunday afternoon, Todd had a full body scan to determine whether cancer had spread to any other parts of his body. It was hard for me to breathe during his scan. I kept praying the cancer was contained. Thankfully, the results showed no evidence of cancer anywhere else in his body. Sunday night, several friends came to visit Todd. We usually met visitors in a hallway so that we didn't overwhelm Todd with too many people crowded in his room at one time. He was still recovering from the long biopsy incision, and he was tired. David and I asked our friends to excuse us for a few minutes so that we could check out the cancer floor. We took the elevator down to the fifth floor and walked through the halls. The first thing I noticed was a ceiling tile painted with the words "Much love to the people who need it, Jona." I immediately started crying. Jona, formerly a sophomore at Todd's school, had lost his battle to cancer the previous year. As I walked through the cancer wing, I didn't see any nurses, I didn't see any patients, and I didn't see any color. All of the halls appeared stark white and were depressing to me. I wanted to go upstairs immediately.

Our friends surrounded us and listened sympathetically as I shared my sadness about leaving our current nurses to go down to the cancer floor. There was nothing they could say to make me feel better, but just having them there with us helped.

The next morning, Todd had port-placement surgery. He would receive his chemo treatments through the port for the next several months. When I saw the rounded port protruding from his thin skin, my heart ached, but Todd didn't seem bothered by it at all. After surgery, Todd was supposed to meet with the radiation doctor. As we waited, he sat in a wheelchair, his back hurting badly, shivering with the cold. I tried not to cry. My heart ached for my precious son and all that he had been through in just a few short days. A nurse came in to check on Todd and to ask whether we needed anything. When I told her how cold he was and how much his back hurt, she immediately moved Todd to a bed. She covered him with a blanket—the kind kept in a warmer. He lay down on that soft bed with the warm blanket and fell right to sleep. When the doctor came in to discuss the radiation process, Todd barely woke up to talk to him. My heart was blessed to know he was finally comfortable.

We were scheduled to move to the fifth floor that day, but I begged several of the nurses not to make us go, telling them I did not like it there.

With compassion in their voices, they all assured me the children's cancer wing was a wonderful place, that the staff on that floor knew what they were doing, and that it was the best place for Todd. Many of them offered me comforting hugs. To make our transition easier, they allowed Todd and me to stay another night on the sixth floor. As Todd slept, I watched him in amazement as I thought back to all he had been through in a few short days. His calmness and acceptance of everything comforted my own heart. I would have understood if I had seen fear or anger in Todd's response to his circumstances, but I was blessed beyond words to see peace.

Brenda Lurtey

Chapter 6

Treatment

The next morning, my eyes brimming with tears, Todd and I moved downstairs to the children's cancer floor. This time I saw nurses at their station and parents walking up and down the hallway with their children, who were obviously cancer patients. There was much more activity on the floor than there had been on Sunday night. The rooms were bigger than the one we had been in, which was nice, but the whole environment still seemed so scary to me. We missed the familiar faces of the sixth floor. Just moments after we settled into our room, two nurses walked in to greet Todd. Katie and Melissa were young and pretty, with big smiles on their faces. They spoke to him with compassion and ease, and I knew immediately that they would take great care of him.

When Todd's first chemotherapy session started, I felt as if I were standing at the bottom of a very large mountain, asking the Lord for a gondola ride to the top. I will never forget watching the nurses hook Todd up to the poison meant to save his life. So many wires and bags had to be attached; I was amazed at their skill and efficiency. As they worked, they made pleasant conversation with Todd. My heart calmed. I decided I shouldn't think of the chemo as poison, but rather as a life-saving liquid. Despite my resolve, I shed a few tears, but I tried to keep them from Todd's view. I would hide my tears many times over the next few months.

Todd's first treatment went pretty well. The nausea medications worked effectively, but Todd still didn't want to eat, and his lack of appetite soon became a big problem. We had been in the hospital for almost a week, and he had not eaten a single full meal—only nibbled a few bites of food here and there.

Within a short time I realized the nurses on the fifth floor had a tender heart for their cancer patients. They did not want them to experience any nausea or pain, and they worked hard to keep them comfortable and make their environment pleasant. They also watched out for the parents. When they noticed me struggling, they offered supportive hugs. The nurses weren't the only people who proved their concern. One of the three oncologists visited Todd every day he was in the hospital. Their dedication and bedside manners impressed me. Dr. Alan, Dr. Nichole, and Dr. Rebecca never rushed with the patients as they made their rounds, they were never grouchy, and they were always ready to listen.

Chemo sessions typically lasted three days. During Todd's first session, we met Charlie, the sweet man who passed out food trays in the hospital. He often served on the children's cancer floor. Todd and I liked Charlie right away. He offered Todd all kinds of food choices. To be honest, the hospital food didn't inspire Todd's taste buds, but thankfully, Charlie had other options. He tempted Todd with ice cream, chocolate milk, jello, chips, and other treats. Even though Todd didn't want to eat, we soon looked forward to Charlie's daily visits. He is one of those hardworking and unassuming people who faithfully work in the background while others get the glory. Some people do great things that the whole world knows about; we put them on a pedestal for everyone to see. Other people work quietly unnoticed, yet what they do is of utmost importance. That is Charlie! He put a smile on children's faces and provided nourishment for kids going through circumstances that some adults, including me, could never handle.

We had one treatment down with possibly eight more to go! By this time Todd had been in the hospital for nearly two weeks, from the biopsy through the first treatment and recovery. Finally, the doctors released Todd. We were going home, but first we had to stop at the orthodontist's office to have Todd's braces removed. After Todd's cancer diagnosis, Dr. Alan advised us to have his braces removed because of all the scans he would need in the future. The idea saddened me because I knew it was not time to take them off. His teeth weren't ready; they would probably just become crooked again. I called the orthodontist's office, told them about Todd's situation, and scheduled a visit. I could see the looks of concern in the staff's eyes when we walked into the office. Typically, after a patient has his braces removed, the staff members cheer and sing a fun song to the patient. Under the circumstances, I was not in the mood for frivolity.

When Dr. Summers took off Todd's braces, he assured Todd his teeth looked beautiful, and he was quite pleased with the results even though he removed the braces early. I agreed. Todd's teeth were perfectly straight, which pleasantly surprised me. A few moments later, the office staff crowded into the room. *"Here we go,"* I thought. Instead of clapping and cheering, they gathered around Todd and one of the staff members began to pray for him. It was the most fitting thing they could have done. When Dr. Summers raised his head, he had tears in his eyes, and so did I.

Over and over again, God showed His grace in Todd's life. In spite of Todd's fragile physical condition, the dark spirit that seemed to come over him in August was now gone. His beautiful smile, enhanced by his straight teeth, had returned despite his cancer. Just as when he was a child, his wide grin blessed us throughout his illness.

Todd went back to school, but he was tired and in pain from the tumor and two surgeries. He had weekly clinic visits at the cancer center between chemo sessions, where they checked his blood counts. If his counts were too low, the oncologist hospitalized him until they came back up. Unfortunately, this happened frequently.

During Todd's second round of chemo, I met Taniesha, another young cancer patient. As I grabbed a drink in the kitchen, a beautiful girl walked into the room. I noticed her bright smile right away. I could see her port, so I knew she was a patient, but what really got my attention was the clam chowder she was heating up. We quickly struck up a conversation. I told Taniesha I could barely get Todd to eat a bite of bread, let alone clam chowder. During our conversation, she told me she was in the hospital for chemo, and after her treatments, she always craved clam chowder. I told her about Todd's cancer diagnosis, how he had no appetite and hadn't eaten for several days. She understood how he felt, but reminded me of how important it was for him to eat so that he would have the nourishment and strength to fight his cancer. Taniesha explained her type of cancer and related that she had recently come out of remission. As she described the disease that was now in her back, my heart ached for her. Silently, I asked the Lord to please heal her and let her live.

When I got back to Todd's room, I told him all about Taniesha. Later that day, the nurses dropped off a kind and encouraging letter from her.

> Hello Todd. My name is Taniesha. I know you don't know me, but I have Rhabdomyoscarcoma. I have been going through treatment to fight this disease for two years. I am in relapse, meaning my cancer has come back. I finished treatment last year and went into remission this past February. This past September, a CT scan showed that my cancer has returned. That is a summary of my cancer story.
>
> I talked to your mom the other night and she told me you aren't eating. When I first started, I wouldn't eat the whole week I was in the hospital. At home I may eat only once a day or bits and pieces of food. But I had to stop doing that because I started losing weight too fast. I understand where you are coming from about eating. I don't know about your religious background, but I have a couple of verses about weathering the storm. This is my storm dealing with cancer once and now having to weather through this storm again. Acts 27:33–36 says, "As day was about to dawn, Paul urged them all to take some food, saying, 'Today is the fourteenth day that you have continued in suspense and without food, having taken nothing. Therefore I urge you to take some food. For it will give you strength, for not a hair is to perish from the head of any of you." And when he had said these things, he took bread, and giving thanks to God in the presence of all he broke it and began to eat. Then they all were encouraged and ate some food themselves." The reason I picked those verses to share with you is because of the message I received from them. We all will have storms. Further in this book the people on this ship make

it out of this storm. By eating a little food they built up strength to get to shore. The storm broke up the ship that they were on, forcing them to use this new strength to survive. They were fasting and becoming weak, but when God appointed Paul to lead them, they ate and became stronger.

My point is that you have to eat so that your body will have the nutrients to fight this chemo and cancer. You need all the strength you can get so that your body can fight off this tumor and still handle the chemo. I'm not trying to tell you what to do, but I wanted to share this with you. I believe you can weather this storm, but remember that you have to feed your body so that it can weather it too. Hope you have a blessed day. –Taniesha

The next day Taniesha came into the room to meet Todd. Her visit couldn't have come at a better time. Todd and I both needed encouragement, and her smile and conversation lifted our spirits. Earlier that morning I had shaved off Todd's hair. For several days, his hair had been falling out all over the bed and the floor, and I knew it was just a matter of time before Todd would be completely bald. I went to the nurses' desk, described what was happening, and asked whether they thought it was time to shave his head. They agreed it was probably a good idea. At first I did not want to do it, but I talked with Todd, and he agreed to let me do the honors. Todd was already used to having me as his barber. I had cut his hair his whole life and had even given him a few buzz cuts, but I had never cut it all off. The entire process took only a minute or two; when I touched the clippers to his head, his hair sloughed off at the roots.

When I finished, Todd immediately checked his reflection in the mirror. His shoulders slouched in disappointment. The loss of his thick, brown hair shocked us both. Fortunately, his nurses came into the room moments later. Enthusiastically, they told him he looked awesome and had a great looking head. Their cheerful attention put a smile on his face.

A couple of Todd's friends had given him some nice skullcaps to wear. When he put on the first cap, he seemed to feel much better. At least he still had his eyebrows and eyelashes.

Throughout Todd's hospital stays, we met a few other children who blessed our lives. One special patient was a precious two-year-old girl named Michaela. She had beautiful, blonde, curly hair and a smile for everyone she met. Michaela had Down Syndrome and had recently been diagnosed with leukemia. My heart went out to her family when they first came up to the cancer floor. I recognized the fear in their eyes, but I knew what they did not yet realize: they were in good hands. Because her treatment plan often required her to stay in the hospital for several weeks at a time, we saw Michaela many times over the next few months.

Todd stayed in bed almost constantly when he was in the hospital, but since Michaela was very young, she had lots of energy. She zipped around the hallways on her little scooter, often stopping by Todd's room to say hello. Todd's family nickname was "Bubba," so we had Michaela call him that too. I loved seeing the smile on Todd's face when she waved to him and called, "Hi Bubba!" as she sat on her scooter outside his door. Today Michaela is a survivor and is cancer free!

Todd and I also enjoyed getting to know Nahemiah. Nahemiah was a young boy about six years old, with a bright smile and big brown eyes. Sometimes he dropped by our room, but occasionally, when Todd felt up to it, he stopped by Nahemiah's room to visit. Nahemiah was a real trooper. Based on his energy level, I would have never guessed he had cancer. Unfortunately, I knew better. The nurses especially loved him and showered him with attention; I often found him perched on the lap of one of the nurses as she worked at the computer.

One day, Nahemiah said, "Let me show you all the Christmas presents I want you to get me." He flipped through a toy catalog and pointed to item after item. How I wished I could buy him all the things he wanted. I had not even had time to shop for my own children, and Christmas was right around the corner.

Chapter 7

New Growth

Before Todd went in for his November chemo treatment, he complained that his shoulder was aching. Dr. Alan looked troubled and ordered a CT scan and ran some other tests to see what could be causing the pain. By this point, I had asked the Lord for just one bit of good news. We needed it; Todd had constant diarrhea, barely ate anything, and just did not feel well. The oncologists decided that Todd should receive TPN, a liquid form of nutrition. I was very relieved that I would no longer have to pressure Todd to eat. I hoped the TPN would give Todd strength and allow him to gain some weight.

After one of his many tests, his nurse, Jenn, told me that Todd tested negative for C-diff. I had no clue what C-diff was, but she assured me it was good news that he didn't have it. I shrugged and thought, *"Ok, Lord, so that was the good news I asked for—thank you, even though I don't know what C-diff is."* Unfortunately, I later learned a lot more about C-Diff than I ever wanted to know.

On the evening of November 19, I turned from watching the city lights through the window to find Dr. John standing at the foot of Todd's bed in his hospital scrubs. He always walked into the room so quietly. From Dr. John's expression, I immediately knew it was not a good thing that he was at the hospital so late. He got right to the point, telling me the results of the CT scan showed the tumor had actually doubled in size and it was wrapped around his vena cava vein. Panicked, I asked, "What are we going to do?"

With concern in his eyes, he told me he really had no choice but to operate and just pick away at the tumor. I wondered why the Lord allowed this to happen. Not only had Dr. John been unable to remove the tumor during the biopsy surgery, but now it was even bigger and more dangerous and required another operation. Thanksgiving was just a few days away, complicating surgical scheduling. We would have to wait to find out what day Todd's surgery would begin.

After Dr. John told Todd the news, he kindly asked, "Todd, do you have any questions?"

"Yes. Did you have a good surgery?"

Dr. John smiled, looked a little surprised, and said, "I did, thank you."

Again, I thought, *"What an unusual question for Todd to ask."* I would have had a million other questions, but not Todd. As always, Todd was the master of random questions. When Dr. John left, I turned to Todd and told him what I wanted to believe in my heart: "Todd, we are just going to have to trust that the Lord knows what He is doing." In reality, I knew it was going to be very difficult for me to trust the Lord through this unexpected change of events.

When I woke up throughout the night and all through the next day, I prayed repeatedly that the Lord would heal my boy. I couldn't get over the troubled look in Dr. John's eyes, and I asked the Lord to please show us if there were any other options. As we waited for surgery, I questioned the Lord over and over again about what He was doing. I tried to let Him know that things were not exactly working out as I had planned. Up to this point, I expected Him to use the chemo to heal Todd. Instead, the tumor had doubled in size and was now even more dangerous; this was certainly not part of my plan! I wondered, though, whether the Lord was going to show Himself even greater now. Maybe He would take an even more impossible situation and heal Todd. That seemed like the logical thing for Him to do. Despite my faith, waiting for God's miracle was agonizing.

Todd seemed unfazed by the news of the tumor's growth. He endured testing and treatment with a courage that I am quite sure I would not have had. Every morning at the crack of dawn, a nurse came in to draw his blood for testing. He also had to urinate in a plastic container so that the nurse could measure his daily output. Many days he was too weak to get out of bed; I had to assist him if he needed to go into the bathroom. Early on, Todd was embarrassed that I had to help him with such personal matters. I wasted no time setting him straight.

Lovingly, I reminded him, "Todd, I am your mom, and I love you no matter what. It's going to have to be you and me working together."

From that time on, I never sensed any more embarrassment, but I did work hard to respect his privacy and dignity, looking away when he actually needed to go to the bathroom. Many times I had to help give him a sponge bath. Fortunately, I had lived with three nursing majors in college, and I remembered their descriptions of bathing patients. I kept Todd covered as much as possible, helped only when necessary, and turned my head when he needed privacy.

Cancer patients endure hardships most of us cannot imagine. I was exhausted both emotionally and physically, and I wasn't even the one with cancer. I was certainly not the one actually going through cancer treatments. Todd's gracious acceptance of everything blew me away. The nurses, pretty and young, asked him every single day about his bodily functions. This would have mortified most teenage boys. Not Todd. It didn't seem to bother him at all. The nurses had been asking Todd for a stool sample for testing, but so far, he had been unable to accommodate them. One day Jenn came in for her normal morning rounds. As she checked Todd's IV bags, he said, nonchalantly, "By the way, I left you a little present in the bathroom." It was such a random comment that Jenn and I burst out laughing. Todd just flashed us his famous grin.

Nights were especially rough in the hospital. Although the nurses moved quietly in and out of our room, our sleep was disrupted. Todd used the urine collector clipped to the side of his bed when he had to relieve himself at night, but sometimes he needed me to get him hand sanitizer from the wall dispenser. Between our unsettled sleep and the news that his tumor had doubled in size, I was emotionally and physically exhausted.

One night I thought I heard Todd slowly climb out of his hospital bed. Normally, I would have asked if he needed help, but I was too tired to lift my head. I thought that he would call out my name if he really needed help. I was cold, but I didn't even have the energy to adjust my covers. Seconds later, I felt someone pulling the blanket over my shoulders. I waited for a moment, and then rolled over to see Todd shuffling away from me. I never spoke a word to him, but my heart overflowed with love. He could barely get out of bed, but he had made the effort to walk over and cover me with a blanket.

The next day, Todd got an unusual burst of energy. He wanted to go to the first floor of the hospital and get some sweet tea from the cafeteria. Other than the previous night, he had not been out of bed for several days, so I definitely wanted him to ride in a wheelchair. He insisted he was strong enough to walk, but I wasn't convinced he could make the long trek without it. We compromised—Todd started out walking, and I brought the wheelchair with us just in case. Todd's nurses were thrilled to see him out of bed; they cheered him on as we passed the nurses' station. When we reached the cafeteria, I asked whether he wanted to sit in the wheelchair.

"No, Mom. I'm fine," he assured me.

I thought, *"Well, there is no use in both of us walking."* Laughing, I climbed into the wheelchair, directing him to hold onto it for support and push me around. As he wheeled me, we spotted Charlie eating his lunch in the cafeteria. He did a double take when he saw Todd was out of bed and pushing me around. He must have thought I was crazy. Quickly, I assured him we had switched places only because Todd refused to ride. We all had a good laugh at Todd's stubbornness. No one looking at the broad smile on Todd's face would have guessed he had such a dangerous tumor growing in his body.

Chapter 8

A Plan

The day before Thanksgiving, David and I met with Dr. Alan, Dr. John, and Amy to discuss the upcoming surgery. I was thankful David was with me. He worked hard to keep up with his job demands and maintain a seminormal routine at home for Brandon, Lauren, and Jeffrey, but I needed his support at this meeting. Once again, the concern in Dr. John's eyes troubled me. During our meeting, Dr. John excused himself from the room to answer his phone. A few moments later, he returned looking visibly relieved. "I'm really glad I took that call."

He explained that the call was from a colleague who is a transplant surgeon in Charleston. Because of the size and location of Todd's tumor, Dr. John was not comfortable doing the surgery in Greenville, so he and the transplant surgeon agreed to have Todd transported to a hospital in Charleston where an experienced team of doctors could remove the tumor.

I felt an immediate peace as the familiar look of confidence returned to Dr. John's eyes. I knew this was the right approach for Todd, and I was grateful for the option, especially since Dr. John's colleague was confident he could remove eighty to ninety percent of the tumor. The hospital arranged to transport Todd by ambulance to Charleston the day after Thanksgiving. As I thought through the plans, I again felt the Lord was about to reveal Himself in a mighty way. Perhaps He did not allow Dr. John to remove Todd's tumor so that He could show an even greater miracle with the removal of an even larger one. Once again, I had it all figured out for the Lord.

That night, Dr. John dropped by Todd's room to say goodbye. As they spoke, I watched their interaction, and it touched me. Obviously, a special bond had formed between them. "I'm really going to be pulling for you, Todd." Dr. John said as he clasped Todd's hand in his own.

Sweet Charlie also came in to say goodbye; he cried as soon as he saw Todd. I tried to comfort him, explaining the surgery in Charleston was a good thing and everything would be all right. Charlie truly loved all the children he helped care for and took his job on the cancer floor seriously.

On Thanksgiving night, my parents planned to sit with Todd so I could eat with David, Brandon, Lauren, and Jeffrey as well as my sister and her family. It was hard for me to leave Todd even for a few hours. I knew he didn't like it when I was away from him. If I stepped out of the room to talk with a friend even for a few minutes, he would usually text me shortly after I left and ask me when I was coming back. When I would step back in the room and ask whether he was all right, he would say, "Yes, I just wanted you." It melted my heart to know that he truly wanted me to be with him. While my heart pulled to stay with Todd, I knew I needed to spend some time with my husband and other children. The days and weeks we had all been apart was hard on our whole family. I also knew my mom would take good care of Todd for the short time I would be at dinner, and I wanted him to spend time with his grandparents. My father was actually a patient in the same hospital, but since he felt better at the time, my mother brought him up to Todd's room in a wheelchair.

As we ate our Thanksgiving meal, we finalized plans for Todd's surgery. The ambulance was scheduled to arrive early in the morning to transport Todd and me to Charleston. David, Brandon, Lauren, and Jeffrey would follow the ambulance so we could all be together for the surgery. My sister, Corinne, and her family also planned to head down later that day. They rented a beach house nearby so that their family and mine would have a place to stay. Although the surgery was going to be rough on Todd, David and I both had peace in our hearts that Charleston was the right location for the surgery to take place.

Chapter 9

Hope Deferred

The next morning, the EMTs arrived to transport Todd. I was relieved to see them walk into our room; I was more than ready to get this tumor out! They strapped Todd onto the stretcher and bundled him up in my warm down comforter. As they wheeled him down the hallway, two of the nurses ran after him, yelling his name. They wanted to hug him and say goodbye. I am not sure whether they thought he would not survive what they knew was a dangerous procedure, but I was confident God would bring him through.

The four-hour trip to Charleston was uneventful. I rode up front with the driver listening to stories about his exciting ambulance runs. Todd rode in the back under continual monitoring by the other EMT. I was so grateful he could ride in the comfort of the ambulance instead of having to sit up in the seat of a car. Halfway through the trip, the driver stopped at a rest area and allowed Brandon to climb in the back with Todd. This kind gesture allowed Brandon to spend some quality time with his brother and gave Brandon the thrill of being in an ambulance.

We arrived at the hospital filled with hope. Todd was transported up to his new room, where a nurse greeted us and took Todd's vitals. Soon, doctors began coming in and out of the room. As each one walked in, I asked whether he or she was Todd's surgeon. I thought, *"Surely the surgeon will be anxious to meet Todd."* Each one seemed to say the same thing: "No, but I will be in the surgery room."

One of the doctors kept talking about her "fellow." It was "my fellow" this, or "my fellow" that. Her words annoyed me. I thought, *"Lady, I don't care about your boyfriend; I just want to speak to the surgeon."* Finally, light dawned, and I realized that at this hospital, they referred to doctors as "fellows."

A few minutes later, yet another fellow came in to evaluate Todd. He told me he was not the head surgeon, but he was a member of the transplant team and would be in the surgery room. I was tired of meeting people who would only be in the room as observers; I wanted specific information from the actual surgeon. I asked the doctor to step out of the room with me, where I questioned him about the specifics of the surgery and Todd's long-term chances of survival. He replied, "I don't know. Your son may die; we'll see." His tone was so nonchalant that he could have been ordering chicken or steak for supper rather than talking about the life of a child. His voice and mannerisms showed me it was no big deal to him whether Todd lived or died. I wondered bitterly whether he would think it no big deal if his child were lying in the hospital bed.

As soon as he left, I lost control and began to weep. I felt so alone; David was with the other kids at the beach house, so he didn't hear the conversation. Later, another fellow or two made the same callous remark that Todd might just die in surgery. Their seeming apathy and the prospect of losing Todd devastated me.

Not long after I heard these negative comments, a young dating couple from our church arrived at Todd's room to drop off dinner for us. Although I had seen them at services, I didn't know Katie and Matt personally, but Todd knew them from their work with his youth group. They were in town visiting Katie's parents for Thanksgiving. Katie's mother, Leeann, and I had attended college together, but I hadn't seen her in years. When they heard Todd's surgery would take place in Charleston, they offered to bring us a meal. I did not have much of an appetite and didn't want to trouble them, but they insisted. Their timing was perfect. Even though they didn't really know me, when they saw my tears, they opened their arms and drew me in for a hug, and then listened compassionately as I tearfully shared all that had happened since we had arrived. Todd was glad to see some familiar faces; seeing his smile lifted my spirits. Even though I hadn't wanted any food, it turned out to be just what I needed. The delicious meal not only nourished my body but also comforted my soul.

When David returned to the hospital, I cried in his arms over the insensitive comments. I missed Dr. John and our oncologists and nurses back home. Our doctors never spoke so callously about Todd's care or the outcome of his treatments. After he comforted me, David sent a text to Amy, Todd's social worker in Greenville, explaining what had happened so far, and told her how much we missed our oncologists back home. He also spoke with some of the nurses at the desk and with a children's social worker at the hospital in Charleston.

With my emotions more in check, I stepped out of Todd's room and talked with one of the first doctors we'd met—the one telling me about her fellow—about how disheartened I was by my conversation with the transplant team member. When I first met her, she was strictly business, but as we spoke, her demeanor grew more compassionate. She apologized for the insensitive comments and then said, "I cannot begin to understand how difficult this situation must be for you and your family. A doctor I had in residency told all of us to remember that "we cut and God heals."

I nodded in agreement. "We absolutely believe God heals, and we are trusting Him to heal Todd. Right now, people all over the world are praying for his healing. When we receive hopeless news, it temporarily takes our focus off the Lord; we just have to get it back where it belongs." I reminded myself that God held Todd in His hands and that He would guide the surgeon.

David and I were told we would meet with the surgeon in charge of Todd's surgery before the end of the day. I was more than ready to discuss matters with him when he finally walked in and announced that he was Todd's surgeon. He looked like a cousin of mine, which I found comforting. I asked him several times whether he was actually going to perform the operation. I needed him to confirm that he was the surgeon, not just one of the fellows. I know he did not have a clue why I kept questioning him. He greeted Todd and talked with him for a few minutes before David and I asked to meet with him privately.

I had already purposed in my heart that I would start out the conversation by telling him we knew the terrible risks and the worst-case scenarios. All we wanted to know was what he felt confident he could accomplish during the surgery. As we sat down, I immediately said, "Before you say anything, I just want you to know that we already know all the bad stuff that could happen with the surgery. We know he can die, so I don't want to talk about that anymore. We want to know what you hope to accomplish."

He gave me a momentary "Lady, you're crazy," look before he confidently replied, "I hope to remove the entire tumor." This was the first positive news we had received since arriving at the hospital. I immediately decided I liked him and appreciated his confidence.

Still, I wanted to assess his ability, so I said, "To put this in terminology that I understand—which is baking terms—you make a wedding cake, and the doctors in Greenville make . . ." I raised my eyebrows waiting for his answer.

He promptly replied, "Cheesecake!" His response gave us all a laugh and lightened the tension in the room.

"If all goes well, you hope to accomplish . . ." I again raised my eyebrows expectantly. He assured us that he was confident in his ability and believed he could remove the entire tumor. He brought his language down to my level, so I felt better after talking to him than after talking to any of his fellows.

Using baking terms when asking about the surgery sounds crazy, but I was beside myself with all the fear the other doctors had put in my heart. I was in "mother bear mode." I was not going to let one more doctor speak in terminology over my head, and I definitely was not going to let one more doctor tell me my child might die on the operating table. I was sleep-deprived and stressed, and my conversation with the surgeon proved it. After he left, I only half-jokingly told a nurse she should put a sign on my door that read "Please do not annoy this mother by giving her any more bad news!"

After my talk with the surgeon and David's talk with the nurses, the hospital staff seemed much more compassionate in their dealings with us. I had to sign consent to operate papers, which included my signature noting that I understood the surgery could result in death. I didn't hesitate. I had already settled that matter in my heart, so signing did not cause me any problems. I knew the Lord was going to bring my boy through this trial.

Todd's operation was scheduled for very early Monday, but the doctor warned us that if an actual transplant surgery arose over the weekend, the hospital would bump Todd's to the next day. I prayed the Lord would allow Todd's surgery to take place as planned.

Todd was still extremely skinny, so I asked the nurse whether they planned to administer the same TPN he received in Greenville. The nurses in Greenville described his TPN as a liquid cheeseburger in a bag, administered through his port. The Charleston nurse informed me that they didn't have orders for TPN, so they could not give it to him. Todd needed nourishment; concerned, I asked God to give Todd a desire to eat actual food. Apprehensively, I asked, "Todd, do you want anything to eat?"

I was overjoyed when he requested a Subway chicken sandwich with bacon and, of course, some sweet tea. I thoroughly enjoyed watching him down the entire sandwich, especially since he had barely eaten the past several weeks. I cherished our time together in those days before surgery—really, I treasured all the time I spent with Todd in the hospital. My job was to walk him through this trial and to remember that he would take his emotional cues from me. Before he went to sleep on Sunday night, he asked, "Mom, are you worried about the surgery?"

"No, Todd, I'm really not. I feel peaceful." I assured him he would be fine because God would take care of him and guide the surgeon's hands.

After Todd fell asleep, Kristen called to see whether I wanted Danny and her to come to Charleston for the surgery. I told her they didn't need to make the drive. Surprised, she asked whether I really meant what I was saying. I did mean it, and told her I knew I could call if I needed them.

I watched Todd sleep for a while, and although I brushed away a few tears, I was calm. I could not do anything for Todd but lay him at the feet of the Lord and trust that He would take care of my precious son and put His healing hands on his body. Everything else was out of my control. Right after I found out about this surgery, I claimed 1 Peter 5:10: "And after you have suffered a while, the God of all grace, who has called you to his eternal glory in Christ, will himself restore, confirm, strengthen, and establish you." All I could say in response was "Lord, please let this be so."

Brenda Lurtey

Chapter 10

A Miracle?

Early Monday morning, David and I followed behind Todd's stretcher as the nurses wheeled him out of his hospital room and into the surgical holding area. Part of me regretted telling Pastor Danny he didn't need to come to Charleston to be with us. His prayers before various surgeries had always brought comfort to our hearts. As I studied Todd, he seemed peaceful as he lay on his bed that morning, and my heart swelled with pride as I watched him patiently endure anything and everything required of him since his cancer diagnosis. Shortly after seven, Todd and several other patients headed to their surgical rooms. The procession looked like a train—patient beds left one right after the other. I had never seen anything like that before. When Todd arrived at his operating room door, we kissed him and told him we loved him. I walked away quickly so that Todd wouldn't see my tears. When the doors shut behind him, a nurse escorted us into a waiting room. It is called a "waiting room" for good reason: you hunker down and wait!

Kristen called a short time later to tell me she and Danny were on their way to Charleston and would be with us in a few hours. With fear in my heart, I asked, "Why is Danny coming? Did God tell him that something bad is going to happen?"

I heard her say, laughing, "Danny, Brenda wants to know if God told you that something bad is going to happen."

He responded that God did not give him any kind of a message; he just wanted to be there for us. What a wonderful pastor the Lord gave to our family. While we waited for Danny and Kristen and for surgical updates, a few local pastors who had heard about our situation came to pray with us, and a friend of mine from Charleston sat with us for a while as well.

Waiting was difficult. Doctors and nurses constantly walked in and out, updating other families on their loved ones' condition. Each time one came in, I held my breath. I knew it was far too soon for them to talk to us; Todd's procedure would take about four hours. Not long after Todd's surgery began, I realized I couldn't stay in the waiting room. I felt too anxious, so David and I went back to Todd's room so that we could rest and try to keep our hearts at peace. While we were there, a sweet lady from the Cancer Society in Charleston visited us. She brought several meal vouchers for our hospital stay, a gas card, and some other presents. This unexpected gift again showed how much the Lord was taking care of our family.

We stayed in Todd's room for a while before heading down to the hallway outside the waiting room to see Danny and Kristen. I still did not want to sit in the waiting room watching doctors come in and out, but I wanted to be close by if they needed us. To pass the time, I read posts sent to the Praying for Todd Lurtey Facebook page friends had created for him. Tears rolled down my cheeks as I read the comments, verses, and reassurances of prayer. Finally, Danny and Kristen walked into the hallway where we waited. I was glad they came after all. Their presence was a tremendous comfort to David and me. While we waited, we talked and prayed.

After about four hours, the surgeon walked up to us and sat down. I think I stopped breathing for a few seconds until he said, "I got it all." We all let out audible sighs of relief. "As expected, I also had to take out the right kidney, the gall bladder, and part of the liver."

Surprised, I asked, "Oh, you had to take the gall bladder?" We knew he might have to take a kidney and part of the liver, but he had never mentioned removing the gall bladder. With a shrug of his shoulders, he said matter-of-factly, "Yeah, it was in my way." His comment made us all laugh.

After the surgeon left, Danny led us in prayer, giving thanks to the Lord for His work. The surgeon's news pleased me, but I wondered why I didn't also feel completely relieved. After the nurses cleaned Todd up and situated him in the ICU, David and I went to be with him. I could hardly wait to see him again. When we came around the curtain to his bed, I wasn't prepared for what I saw. Todd looked emaciated, his eyeballs bulged out, and they were fluttering; he didn't seem fully awake. Tubes ran everywhere, including one going down his throat and one up his nose. Although my desire was to grab him in my arms, he looked so fragile that I was afraid even to touch him. Thankfully, the ICU nurse stayed right there keeping him comfortable and jotting down notes about his condition.

The surgeon came in a short time later and asked me how I thought he looked. I mouthed the words, "He looks awful!"

He looked surprised and said, "Why? I think he looks great!"

I responded, "Well, I'm used to seeing him sleep like this." I put my hands beside my cheek as a small child sleeps. "Not like this." I pointed to Todd in the hospital bed. His chest appeared to rise and fall more rapidly than usual, and his breathing seemed labored.

As Todd regained consciousness, he slapped at my hand and pointed to the tube in his mouth. Leaning over, I asked, "Do you want them to take it out?" He nodded yes. I tried to keep him calm as I assured him the nurse would remove the tubes as soon as she could. Finally, she unhooked some of the tubes and pulled the one out of his throat.

Todd searched my eyes and in a hoarse voice spoke his first words, "Mom, can you tell me what Jesus did for me?"

I choked up. "The surgeon got the whole tumor!"

Todd replied only one word. "Oh." He closed his eyes and smiled as a few happy tears slipped down his cheeks. It was not a nonchalant response, but a relieved one. This was the first time I saw Todd shed tears throughout his whole ordeal to this point. He had not cried when he learned he had cancer or even when Dr. John told us the tumor had doubled in size.

Todd had to remain in the ICU for two days, so I couldn't spend the night. I hated leaving him. I always stayed with him at the hospital, but here there was no place for me to sleep. The nurses assured me that they would take good care of him, so David and I went to the beach house. I tried to get a good night's sleep, but I could not completely relax because my heart was with Todd.

Early the next morning, David and I headed back to the hospital. I was happy to be reunited with Todd, and I was thankful the nurses told me he had a pretty good night. I knew he was in quite a bit of pain from the surgery and he was very thirsty, but because of the extensive surgery, he was not allowed to eat or drink anything. All I could do was swab his mouth with water. I was so glad I had some exciting news to share with him. My brother, Brent, affectionately referred to as "Uncle Bunny" by all his nieces and nephews, was flying in from South Africa. David and the kids had to return to Greenville for work and school later that day. Brent would stay with me so that I would not have to be alone. The look on Todd's face when his Uncle Bunny walked up to his bed in ICU was priceless. Todd loved his uncle, and I knew his presence would help Todd's recovery. Since Todd had to remain in ICU for another night, I was glad Brent could drive me to the place I would be staying that evening.

Thanks to the kindness of the Cancer Society, Brent and I ate free meals at the hospital for the rest of the week. For a family struggling with medical bills, the meal vouchers were a huge blessing. During the day Brent, Todd, and I watched Andy Griffith reruns, and we enjoyed just being together. I could tell Todd was in quite a bit of pain, and I ached for him. The surgeon was concerned about fluid around Todd's lungs, so they inserted a small bulb for drainage. That seemed to help, but it was yet another in a long line of surgical procedures, and it made him sore. Todd was terribly thirsty and wanted water, but he still couldn't drink that whole day. I could only swab his mouth. He wasn't hungry, but since he couldn't have any food anyway, this time his lack of appetite was a good thing. I tried not to think about how much weight he could be losing. His last meal had been Sunday night, and it was now Tuesday.

On Wednesday the surgeon wanted Todd up and walking, and he wanted him to be moved to a regular room. I was okay with the regular room because I wanted to stay with him again, but the walking part made me want to cry for him. I wondered how in the wide world this poor kid, who winced in pain whenever the staff moved him even slightly, could walk. The nurses quietly told me that if they could get him from the ICU bed to a regular room bed, they would consider that his accomplishment for the day. Moving Todd to a regular room took nearly everything out of him, but at least Uncle Bunny was there to provide support and comic relief that helped us both.

Since Brent couldn't stay at the hospital with us, he slept in a prophet's chamber at a church about twenty minutes from the hospital. A prophet's chamber is a place that a person or church provides for someone in need. The concept is based on 2 Kings 4:8 and 10: "Elisha went on to Shunem, where a wealthy woman lived, who urged him to eat some food. So whenever he passed that way, he would turn in there to eat food. And she said to her husband, . . . Let us make a small room on the roof with walls and put there for him a bed, a table, a chair, and a lamp, so that whenever he comes to us, he can go in there." The prophet's chamber was clean, inviting, and, most important, another example of God's repeated provision.

Brenda Lurtey

Chapter 11

A Gondola Ride to the Top

On Thursday, the surgeon told Brent and me that he wanted Todd to go home on Friday. I thought he had lost his mind. Todd still hadn't walked at all, and I didn't know how in the world I could take care of him. The incision in his abdomen looked like a huge Mercedes symbol covering most of his stomach. Frankly, the responsibility of caring for him scared me to death. The surgeon made me feel better about the decision when he reminded me that a hospital is full of germs, so Todd would be safer at home. At least that made sense.

I was ready to leave the hospital and get some real rest. Although I fell asleep quickly at night, nurses on their rounds constantly interrupted our sleep. In addition, since the facility is a teaching hospital, large groups of medical students gathered outside our door in the wee hours of the morning, having class, and discussing their "tumor patient."

The only milestone Todd had to cross before leaving the hospital was a walk from his room to the end of the hall. I could not believe my eyes as I watched my son, who had been through so much, shuffle down the long hallway. Despite everything he'd been through, he was determined to accomplish this last task. Brent and I cheered him on and so did the nurses!

During the discharge process, I privately asked the surgeon whether he thought the tumor would grow right back and whether or not Todd would die. He confidently responded, "No, I expect him to go on and lead a full and healthy life." I guess in his mind, since he had removed the entire tumor, Todd would finish his chemotherapy treatments, and that would be the end of his cancer. Again, I was bothered that his statement did not make me feel completely relieved, but I tried not to dwell on my doubts.

Normally, they would have asked us to come back to Charleston for follow-up visits, but since Dr. John was a colleague, the surgeon released Todd to Dr. John's care. This was an unexpected blessing, because the logistics of getting Todd back and forth to Charleston were daunting.

I worried about surgical complications, so Todd, Brent, and I spent two nights at the prophet's chamber so that we could remain near the hospital before undertaking the three-hour journey home. As God would have it, Todd's high school basketball team and cheerleaders were at the church school where the prophet's chamber was located. Coincidence? Not to me. God had this in His plan all along. Todd was eager to see some of his friends and wanted to surprise them in the gymnasium. As I gingerly pushed Todd in the wheelchair across the bumpy gravel road, a church member rushed up and offered the church's golf cart to transport Todd between the prophet's chamber and the gymnasium. We quickly loaded the wheelchair in the back of the cart and drove the rest of the way to the gym. The cart was the perfect mode of transportation.

The guys were in the middle of the game when I wheeled Todd into the gym. When they caught a glimpse of him, they turned their heads and yelled out his name in delight. At half time, he was the superhero of the day. Cheering, the players and cheerleaders ran over and smothered him with hugs. I cringed, hoping no one would hurt him at his incisions, yet my heart was thrilled as I saw Todd's joy and the joy of his classmates. I struggled to hold back my tears. Todd's classmates were thankful God had answered their prayers. I began to relax and allow myself to think, *"Maybe the Lord really did give us all the miracle we prayed for."*

When Todd got into his bed that evening, I nervously wondered what I would do if something happened to him during the night. Seeing Todd curled up in that big bed, free from monitors and tubes was a joy. He seemed so comfortable and peaceful. As I thought back on all that had taken place over the last week, my heart swelled with thankfulness that he had come through the surgery. In just a few days, we would go home. The Lord had answered our prayers; the cancer journey lay behind us. In a way, I felt as if the Lord had given me the gondola ride to the top of the mountain that I had prayed for.

Chapter 12

Weight Loss

Although the surgery was a success, the entire experience took a huge toll on Todd's body. I noticed as never before how deathly skinny he was, and his frailty concerned me. When we went to our cancer clinic for his normal checkup and he stepped on the scale, my heart sank. He weighed eighty-three pounds with all of his clothes on, including jeans and a jacket! He knew his weight was too low. He immediately looked over at me with fear in his eyes, waiting to see my reaction. I tried to smile. "Don't worry, Todd," I said. "Dr. Alan will help you and take good care of you."

His oncologist was as kind as ever. He assured Todd he was happy he'd come through the surgery and he would help him with his weight and nutrition. Since Todd was recovering from major surgery, we requested that Dr. Alan delay his next chemo treatment until January. We wanted his body to recover from all the procedures, and we hoped he would gain some weight. Dr. Alan thought it would be all right to delay the chemo treatment, but he decided to admit Todd into the hospital where they could supplement and monitor his nutritional intake. Before we left the clinic to check into the hospital, I snapped a picture of Dr. Alan and Todd together. Whenever I look at that picture, it reminds me of the hope and joy we had in our hearts at that time.

Being back in our hometown with our oncologists and nurses, and on our cancer floor, was wonderful. As the staff saw him again, they greeted us with hugs and looks of relief that he had survived his huge surgery. Charlie and Dr. John each came to see Todd and welcome him home. Dr. John suggested we allow him to insert a feeding tube to help with Todd's nourishment. He worried weight would continue to be an issue for Todd during his treatments. David and I agreed with his assessment. Todd had no appetite, so we constantly nagged him to eat. The tube would take pressure off him when he did not feel like eating. Todd could not stand to lose any more weight.

As per Dr. John's advice, Todd had his feeding tube placed on December 12 during yet another surgery. We hoped that now Todd was truly on the road to recovery. Feeding tube placement is considered a minor surgery, and the tube itself should have caused only temporary discomfort, but it seemed to bother Todd all the time. The skin surrounding the feeding tube was sore, and he could feel the tube flicking around on the inside. He did not want anyone to touch it. On December 17, Todd had another surgery to replace the initial feeding tube with one that the doctors hoped would be more functional for him.

Todd's nutritional needs required us to have an extended hospital stay. It was during this time that Todd contracted Clostridium difficile or what's more commonly known as C. diff for short. C. diff is an infection in the colon caused by bacteria. The symptoms of C. diff are fever, diarrhea, and abdominal pain. Todd was not contagious to me, but he was highly contagious to the other children on the floor, so we were quarantined. Although the nurses weren't at risk for contracting C. diff, they could easily pass it along to the other children on the floor whose immune systems were compromised. Everyone entering our room had to gown up completely and wash their hands upon entering and leaving the room. Nurses, doctors, and hospital workers came in and out of our room all day long. Each time, it was the same story: gown up and wash your hands. I felt sorry for them. There were times when, just after they had removed their gowns after leaving our room, an alarm would sound on Todd's chemo machine, indicating a bubble in an IV line. They would come back, gown up, take care of the bubble—sometimes in just a minute or two—remove the gown, wash their hands, and leave again. Our trash can overflowed with disposable blue gowns. Once a patient contracts C. diff, he is considered contagious in a hospital setting for a month. Todd's room had a sign on his door warning people to stop and gown up before entry. I felt like we had the plague!

During this hospital stay, the Lord brought a new friend into my life. I had asked David to go to the Kmart across the street from the hospital to buy Todd a blanket he could always have with him when he went in for a chemo treatment. It would forever be called his "chemo blanket." David searched the store shelves until he found a soft brown blanket with an equally soft and fleecy white fabric on the other side. While at Kmart, David ran into a couple he recognized as our church's missionaries to Cameroon, West Africa. Walter and Carol were back in the States for a few months visiting family and friends. David introduced himself to Walter and Carol and mentioned that Todd was in the hospital. I was blessed when many months later Carol shared her thoughts on our meeting that day.

> A casual moment or a simple errand can crystalize in time if we encounter something marvelous in the mundane. I cannot recall why my family and I stopped by Kmart one cold evening, but I will never forget encountering David Lurtey near the cash registers. David had dashed to the department store to purchase a warm blanket for Todd, and he recognized my family. He greeted us and mentioned the purpose for his errand.

> "Neurofibromatosis" is not a word that one hears in daily conversation, and my interest was sparked. I had studied Von Recklinghausen disease in medical school and encountered it in Cameroon, West Africa, but I was surprised to hear that David's son Todd was hospitalized secondary to complication of that disorder. Todd's father was friendly and greeted us warmly, but I knew that he was shouldering a tremendous burden given the circumstances surrounding his son. I left Kmart with a desire to visit the hospital and to spend some time with Brenda, Todd's mother. I also wanted to meet Todd, but I didn't want to bother him. I assumed that Todd had already seen more doctors than he would have cared to meet!

Brenda and I prayed for Todd in the lobby of the hospital, and she encouraged me visit Todd in his room. She led the way to the pediatric oncology floor and then into Todd's room. When Brenda introduced me to Todd, the most remarkable smile met my gaze. Disarmed by his smile, I did not notice his thin frame, IV lines, or chest tube until after we had exchanged greetings. I told Todd that I would continue to pray for him, and I meant it.

When I visited Todd during a subsequent hospitalization, he was in more pain—being greatly bothered by a feeding tube. He was extremely thin, but his smile was unchanged. Todd's sweet submission to suffering made a lasting impression on me. God, in His providence, had a purpose in a "chance encounter" in Kmart! I joined a host of other friends who followed Todd and his amazing family during a journey that touched us all.

Not long after our initial meeting, Carol and her family returned to Africa, but she continued to encourage me by email. Many days when sadness threatened to overwhelm me, the Lord prompted Carol to send a long letter reminding me that she was thinking about me and praying for our family. I feel blessed to know Carol and I have gained a faithful prayer warrior and a true friend. What touches me is that in the two short encounters Carol had with Todd, the Lord used Todd's circumstances to touch her life. This has shown me that the Lord does not solely use our life story to bring Him honor when things are going well; He often chooses to use our life story in the midst of a personal storm.

Chapter 13

A Brief Period of Respite

Christmas was fast approaching, and we prayed we would not have to spend the holidays in the hospital. Thankfully, Todd was released a few days before Christmas. I didn't care whether I received any Christmas presents at all. I had already been given the greatest gift I could ask for at that point. Todd was alive, his tumor was gone, and our family would spend Christmas together at home. But just as the Lord had watched over Todd all throughout his illness, He also had His hands on our family as a whole. Back in November, my friend Jenny told me that many people wanted to help our family, but they didn't know what we needed. I couldn't think clearly, so I didn't know what help to ask for. Finally, a thought occurred to me and I said, "I don't have any Christmas gifts for my kids."

Todd had been in and out of the hospital for such a long time, and my life revolved around caring for him. I explained this to Jenny, and she replied, "I'm on it!"

I thought just she was going to buy presents for my children, but to my great surprise, she and several other friends bought an abundance of gifts for our whole family. We had more presents that Christmas than we had ever had in years past. Not only were we showered with gifts from close friends, the Caringbridge organization in Charleston also sent an abundance of gifts to our family. Strangers sacrificially gave of themselves to make sure we all had presents for Christmas. We loved everything we received, but much more important, we loved the kindness and thoughtfulness behind the gifts. We took a few minutes to pray for the people who had ministered to our family and asked God to bless everyone who made our Christmas special. As I looked at all four of my children sitting on the couch that day, I was overwhelmed with thankfulness. Todd was smiling, and I was thankful to see them all together once more. My heart was full.

David and I did manage to buy one very special gift for our children. I had always told the kids that if I ever found a female golden retriever puppy, I would get her for them. I jokingly, yet seriously, warned David about my intentions. He knew that one day the inevitable would happen. In November, I told Amy, Todd's hospital social worker, how much I would love to get Todd and the other kids a golden retriever. Christmas was coming up and they really didn't need anything, but they had always wanted a dog. She made some phone calls and found a breeder. I contacted the breeder and learned her dog had just birthed a litter of eleven puppies.

With a small amount of reluctance on David's part and joy on mine, we sneaked away to see the new puppies. The puppy I held fit in the palms of my hands. With a generous gift of money from some friends, we decided to put a down payment on her and let the kids know on Christmas Day that they would be getting a dog in the near future.

Brandon, Todd, Lauren, and Jeffrey were thrilled with all of the gifts that our friends had generously showered on them. David and I told them we had one more special gift for them. We showed them a picture of the puppy that was soon to belong to them, and it was the icing on the cake! They yelled and cheered, and we were all overwhelmed by the Lord's abundant blessings to us. The day after Christmas, we drove to the breeder's house so that they could at least hold their new dog; she was not yet ready to be weaned from her mother. Eleven balls of fur—looking exactly alike—ran up to my kids. Few things are cuter than a golden retriever puppy. The breeder knew exactly which one she had saved for us, and the kids took to her immediately. I actually missed our puppy in the days between visiting her at the breeder's and the day she came home to live with us.

A few days after Christmas, as we so often did, our family went to Dollywood, our favorite vacation spot in Tennessee. Although Todd was feeling better, he was still weak, so we pushed him through the park in a wheelchair. In spite of his weakness, he managed to get out of the wheelchair long enough to enjoy all his favorite rides—including the newest roller coaster. Our friends Barry and Carol and their two children, Christine and Brandon, met us in Tennessee, and our families had a great time eating together, exploring Gatlinburg in the snow, and laughing more than we had laughed in weeks. We made wonderful memories in those few days. Seeing Todd enjoy life after all he had been through was a blessing. The feeding tube really hurt him, though. He ate a little bit of food here and there, but not nearly enough, so the extra nutrition from the feeding tube was crucial. He also got his medicine in liquid form through the tube and didn't have to swallow horse pills anymore!

Soon after we came home from our Dollywood trip, David picked up our rambunctious new puppy. We named her Gracie to remind us of God's continual grace throughout Todd's ordeal. Brandon, Todd, Lauren, and Jeffrey all adored Gracie. I loved seeing the joy on their faces as they played with their brand new puppy. Even David, though apprehensive at first, seemed to enjoy the newest member of our family. Gracie often cuddled next to Todd while he rested on the couch. It seemed as if the hardest part of Todd's illness was behind us and, maybe, just maybe, life would get back to normal.

Brenda Lurtey

Chapter 14

Complications and New Pain

On January 4, Todd was admitted to the hospital for his first chemo treatment since the surgery. We wanted to get one treatment out of the way before the start of second semester, which would begin just a few days after the treatment ended. In the past, I had prayed constantly for Todd's healing, but I hadn't really prayed that he wouldn't have any complications during his chemo sessions. This time I prayed everything would go well and his stay would be uneventful. We seemed to have passed through our greatest trial; little did I know what was to come in the weeks and months ahead.

Although Todd tolerated his chemo well, he again tested positive for C. diff, which meant we were under isolation during the three-day hospital stay. In addition, Todd's feeding tube clogged, requiring surgery to replace it. Although Todd's weight had slightly improved as a result of the feeding tube, he still struggled with a lack of desire for food. He rarely wanted food, but he always craved sweet tea.

With the start of second semester, I was determined to help Todd stay caught up in school even during chemo sessions. Fortunately, he had an easy schedule, and we lived close enough to school that he could come home for a long period between his morning and afternoon classes. Despite the undemanding schedule, Todd barely attended school during January.

On January 13 Todd was again admitted to the hospital because of low blood counts and pain associated with his feeding tube. We remained in the hospital for five days. During this time I tried my best to get him to do his schoolwork, but he never had the strength to complete any assignments. His guidance counselor told me just to concern myself with helping Todd get through the treatments; she would take care of helping him with his schooling. The days in the hospital were long and sometimes lonely, but I loved spending that time with Todd. He didn't talk very much, but he always wanted me in the room with him, and I was happy that we could be together.

On January 25, the plan was for Todd to be admitted to the hospital for three days. It would be his second chemo treatment since the tumor was removed. Hopefully, he would feel well enough to go back to school a day or so later. God had very different plans in store for our family.

During this hospital stay Todd began to have a slight cough and runny nose, and we were still on C-diff precautions for a few more days. An x-ray revealed a large amount of fluid around his lungs. Todd went into surgery yet again, this time to have a chest tube inserted. As soon as he came out of the operating room, I joined him in recovery. As I hugged him, he pulled me close and cried; telling me the doctor didn't put him to sleep during the procedure. Todd insisted the doctor inserted the chest tube while he was awake. I said, "No, he didn't, honey. I saw you—you were asleep when the surgery began."

The anesthesiologist quietly told me, "Todd did start to wake up during the procedure, but his blood pressure dropped very low, and we weren't able to give him any more medicine."

I felt terrible. Seeing the chest tube made me sad for him as well. I had not realized it would be so big. I thought it was just going to be like the small bulb and tube he had in recovery in Charleston. Instead, this was a much larger one going into a big box on the floor. Dr. John told me that as soon as he inserted the tube, two liters of fluid immediately drained out from around Todd's lungs, causing the drop in blood pressure. His description scared me. Over the next few days, I watched the box constantly. I knew the amount of fluid still draining out was not good. The excessive drainage puzzled the doctors too.

Todd continued having diarrhea from the C. diff, and he began throwing up green bile. By this time, his counts from the chemo were very low, so we were stuck in the hospital for a while.

To make matters worse, Todd's shoulder began hurting again, and he had a lot of abdominal pain. Dr. Alan ordered another CT scan. That worried me. I wanted him to assure me it was nothing; but I had learned to read the concern in his eyes, and I knew it was not going to be "no big deal." In the midst of waiting for his counts to go up and watching Todd's physical body suffer, I noticed an unfamiliar sadness settle over Todd's spirit. The only window in his room looked into a lobby, so we had to keep the blinds shut. We both needed sunshine and a bigger room, so I requested a room change as soon as possible.

The results of the CT scan revealed a possible tumor recurrence, but it was questionable. Dr. John informed me that he sent the scans to the Charleston surgeon for review. The surgeon discussed Todd's case with the tumor board in Charleston, but he also wanted another doctor to review the scans before making a definitive assessment. My heart was so heavy. Once again, the wait was agonizing.

Brenda Lurtey

Chapter 15

Trial of Faith

I will never forget the night Dr. John came to Todd's room to give us his test results. Unfortunately, results always seemed to come when I was alone. Early in Todd's illness, David and I agreed that I would stay with Todd and David would keep things together at home. This meant David was not with us at the hospital very often. Dr. John greeted Todd, and then he and I left the room so that we could speak privately. My world changed completely at that moment. Dr. John stood before me in his green scrubs with such a look of compassion on his face. Gently, he advised me that what they saw on the scan appeared to be another tumor. This time it seemed to be in the vena cava. I could not believe what I was hearing. I silently prayed, *"Lord, what are you doing?"* I didn't know what else to say to the Lord. I didn't know what questions to ask Dr. John. He asked whether David was with me. Crying softly, I shook my head. I knew David did not want me to be alone when I heard bad news, so I asked Dr. John to please call David when he had any more information about the tumor and what the new plan would be for Todd's treatment.

With tears welling in his eyes, Dr. John said, "You have a remarkable son and a remarkable family." His compassion touched my heart. I felt sad for him; he always had to deliver bad news to us. I knew that had to be hard for him.

Dr. John and I walked back into Todd's room where we shared with him that another tumor was growing. We kept the information as basic as possible: Dr. John was in touch with the surgeon in Charleston, and we were all waiting for a decision to be made about any new treatment options. Todd was somewhat prepared for the news. Earlier, I had told him the doctors suspected they saw another tumor. When Todd and I were alone, he shed only a tear or two and then searched my eyes for my reaction. I reminded him that God never allows us to suffer in vain, that He had a plan for all this, and that He loved Todd very much. What else could I say? I was stunned myself, and I was searching for my own answers.

Although I tried to be brave on the outside, there was a battle going on in my heart between what I knew to be true—that God never allows us to suffer in vain and He has everything under control—and the hopeless words Satan whispered to me:

"God doesn't know what He's doing. Everything is a mess. You're all alone. Todd is going to die. There is no hope."

I told Todd that because I was his mom and because I loved him, I couldn't help crying. He watched TV while I held his hand, prayed, and cried—silently, just as I had that night on the hotel balcony when Todd was a little boy.

"Lord, help, I need someone. David is with the other kids, and I am all alone."

God answered my plea almost immediately. Moments later, Kristen and Danny walked into the hospital room. Danny had actually already come to pray with Todd earlier in the day but left because he was supposed to preach in our mid-week prayer meeting that night.

I lifted my head with tears still rolling down my cheeks. "What are you doing here? Aren't you supposed to be at church?"

Danny answered, "I asked one of the elders to take the service because I knew we were needed here with you and Todd." Kristen gathered me in her arms for a hug. I immediately felt calmer just having them there. We left Todd's room and went to a private area where I told them everything I knew up to that point. We prayed together and asked the Lord for strength and wisdom as we waited for God to show us the next step.

A day or so later, Todd and I moved to a bigger room with a window. Sunshine really does a body good. As an added surprise, snow—something we don't get regularly in South Carolina—was falling lightly just beyond the window. I opened the blinds so that Todd could enjoy the flakes mixed with rays of sunshine. The sadness left Todd's countenance almost immediately; I never saw it return.

Todd continued throwing up green bile and suffering from pain associated with his shoulder and the feeding tube. The toll on his body was devastating, but we could do nothing but wait for a decision from the doctors about how to treat the tumor. I could not figure out how everything would work out for Todd. I dreaded the thought of going back to Charleston for another surgery, and if we did, I didn't see how Todd could possibly survive.

My heart battled with the reality that Todd seemed to be dying and the fact that I needed to have faith that God would heal him. For months I had watched my precious son suffer. Every day I put on a brave face for Todd, while inside my heart ached with fear and the uncertainty of the future. I read the concern on the doctors' faces as they came into Todd's room and saw his condition.

David tried to come see us every day, but he sometimes ran late because of work and responsibilities at home. When he did show up, after greeting Todd and me, he often headed to the cafeteria for a quick supper. Honestly, I grew angry at him, not only for being late but also for thinking about food when our situation seemed so bleak. I knew Satan wanted to exploit Todd's illness to destroy our marriage, and I resolved to prevent that from happening. Instead of allowing resentment to control me, I thought, *"David doesn't know how I feel, and he doesn't understand how bad the situation is, so instead of being angry, I am going to tell him exactly what's going on."*

The next time David came to visit, I asked him if we could talk privately. We went into a waiting area, where I shared the burdens of my heart. "David, I feel like Todd is dying, and I'm bearing all the bad news by myself. I need you here and Todd needs you."

The look on his face confirmed I was right; he didn't understand the bleakness of Todd's situation. As we talked, he lovingly assured me that he would support Todd and me more with his physical presence and help me bear my burdens, because they were really our burdens. From that point on, he arrived at the hospital when he said he would, and he made sure that the doctors called him with news about the tumor. I was thankful God led me to share my hurt with David rather than let Satan use my anger to drive a wedge between us. I looked forward to his visits every day.

Waiting for news was difficult. When the oncologists came in on their daily rounds, they told me the same thing: they were not exactly sure what they were looking at on the scans. When David came to visit us, I searched his eyes and asked, "Did you hear anything from Dr. John?"

Every day his response was the same. "Not yet."

I wanted answers, but at the same time, I hoped no news was good news. I felt as if I was on an emotional rollercoaster. Finally, I told David that whenever he came in the hospital room, I needed him to come in with his thumbs up, showing me everything was okay. I didn't want to wait for him to tell me; I wanted to know immediately. David humored me, and the next few times he came into Todd's room, I saw his "thumbs up" from the other side of the privacy curtain before I even saw his face. A few days later, though, he walked into the room with a pitiful expression on his face. Stunned, I realized he hadn't come in with his thumbs up.

We went into the laundry room of the cancer floor—my meeting place when I needed to talk to someone in private. Gravely, David told me Dr. John had called and requested a meeting. Dr. John didn't tell him much during their phone conversation, only that the news was not good. Something terrible was happening, and our hearts felt sick waiting for that meeting to start.

Chapter 16

Devastating News

When Todd's doctors were available, we all gathered in the parents' lounge, a place I now refer to as the "bad news room." Dr. John, Dr. Nichole, Dr. Rebecca, and Amy joined David and me. With a sympathetic voice, Dr. John told us Todd had tumor progression in the vena cava and throughout the vascular system despite receiving high doses of chemotherapy. It did not seem that offering Todd any further treatments would be of benefit to him, and he was too weak to endure another major surgery. He suspected Todd would suffer a catastrophic death. I asked, "What do you mean by catastrophic?"

Dr. John responded, "Todd might have a heart attack, or the vena cava could rupture."

He continued talking, but at that point I lost the ability to comprehend any other words that were said. All I understood was that my baby was going to die. David and I cried, not angry tears, just tears from broken hearts. Turning to Dr. John I asked, "How long will he live?"

"With chemo, maybe a year. Without chemo, maybe a month or two—it could even be a day or two."

All the doctors looked at David and me with such compassion in their eyes. They were not dealing with a "patient"; they were dealing with our son Todd. I believe they all deeply cared about him and our family, and they were distressed at having delivered such devastating news. Once again, God revealed His promise when He gave me a peace that surpassed my understanding. My heart was breaking, but I knew the Lord was with me.

As different ones were talking, I thought of something that made me smile, and I knew I wanted to share it with everyone. I asked Amy and the doctors whether they could use a laugh, because I had a random Todd story to tell. They all looked surprised at my comment yet nodded their consent.

I recalled one early morning during our hospital stay when I chatted quietly with Nurse Lisa while she changed Todd's chemo bags. She understood what David and I were going through. Her daughter Melissa had leukemia when she was five. Now as a adult survivor, Melissa was also a nurse working on Todd's cancer floor. As Lisa and I talked, I looked over at Todd. I didn't necessarily want him to hear our conversation. His mouth was hanging wide open, and he appeared fast asleep. I softly asked Lisa whether her daughter had lost her eyebrows and eyelashes during chemo, because I could tell Todd's were falling out. Without opening his eyes, Todd piped up in a weak voice, "I think Dr. John has a unibrow."

The story brought fits of laughter from everyone in the "bad news room," including Dr. John, but especially from his female colleagues. I had never noticed Dr. John's eyebrows before, but apparently Todd had paid attention to them. I fear Dr. John will never get over the playful ridicule. I will always remember that scenario and thank the Lord that, once again, one of Todd's random comments brought joy even in the midst of devastating news.

Our laughter was brief because there were still serious issues to discuss. David and I decided that rather than allow Todd to continue chemo or to die in the hospital, we wanted to take him home. I asked Dr. John to remove the feeding tube because it caused Todd a tremendous amount of pain and it was clogged once again. We also made the difficult decision to sign do not resuscitate forms in the event Todd passed away at home and emergency medical services had to be called. With this signed form, they would not be required to intervene. Amy told us she would call us on Monday to discuss setting up hospice.

As David and I walked back to Todd's room, neither one of us knew exactly what we were going to say to Todd or how we would say it. How do you tell your child there is no hope for him to live? How do you tell him cancer is going to win? How do you come to grips with a devastating report, yet trust God for healing? We decided to keep our information as basic yet as truthful as possible. We confirmed the tumor had grown back and that there was nothing more that could be done in the hospital. We were taking him home. Above all, we spoke the words we knew were true even if we did not feel it in our heart. We reminded him that our times are in God's hands. He was not going to die a moment earlier than God had planned before the beginning of time, so we had nothing to worry about. It seemed as if the only words Todd heard were that we were taking him home. Just then, Pastor McCormick, our assistant pastor, walked into the room. He and David briefly stepped out so that David could fill him in on the current situation.

While David was gone, Dr. John came in to remove Todd's chest tube and feeding tube. It was remarkable and touching to me that just a few months earlier, Dr. John had stood at the foot of Todd's bed, a stranger, delivering the terrible news that he had cancer. This day was different in many ways. Although the news he had earlier delivered to us about Todd was the worst news yet, Dr. John was no longer a stranger. Todd looked into his eyes with a bit of fear, yet trust, while Dr. John looked at him with eyes full of compassion. He stood at Todd's side with his hand on Todd's. Dr. John was no longer just a surgeon; he had become a friend.

Right before he began removing the tubes, David and Pastor McCormick came back into the room to pray for the procedure and for Todd. Dr. John offered to step out, but Pastor McCormick asked him to stay and join us. We gathered around Todd's bed, held hands and prayed for God's will to be done in Todd's life.

I left the room while Dr. John removed the tubes—he was finished in a matter of minutes. Todd had tears running down his cheeks when I came back into the room. Gently, I asked, "What's the matter, honey?" His comment shocked me.

"Mom, I don't hurt anymore, and it's been a really long time since I felt this way."

I was still reeling from all the devastating news we had just received during our meeting, yet I wondered briefly whether the feeding tube had caused all of Todd's recent problems. I could not think clearly about anything except that the doctors had just told me our precious son was going to die.

Brenda Lurtey

Chapter 17

Discharge

Normally, discharge can require an hour or more. Not this time; we left in a frenzied hurry. It was too fast, really. David and I did not have adequate time to say goodbye to the nurses or thank them for their compassionate care. I hugged Dr. John but didn't have the words to convey my gratitude for all that he had done for Todd. It was the same with the oncologists and Amy, Todd's social worker. How do you adequately thank the people that tried desperately to save your child's life? We hugged the nurses, but couldn't speak any of the words of love or appreciation that were in our hearts. I was not convinced Todd completely understood why we were going home, but he seemed peaceful and relieved to be leaving the hospital. Dr. Nichole helped me bring Todd down to the front of the hospital. He sat passively in his wheelchair while I pulled the car up to the hospital door. The hospital teemed with life— new mothers left with their infants, doctors and nurses hustled by, and families chatted and laughed as they passed. All around us, life went on, while mine felt as if it were ending. None of the people hurrying by knew I was taking my child home to die. The sun was shining, but the world seemed dark to me. I hugged Dr. Nichole goodbye but couldn't speak.

As I drove home, I tried hard not to cry in front of Todd. He seemed happy to finally be out of the hospital after two long weeks of waiting. When we got home, Todd immediately asked for something to eat and drink. It was not much, but it was something. For the rest of the day, he sat up on the couch in our family room while I lay beside him with my head in his lap, gripping his hand in mine. Tears streamed unchecked down my cheeks.

Under the circumstances, Todd probably should have cried or at least acted depressed, but the opposite was true. His smile stretched across his face from ear to ear. He was home, and that was all that mattered to him. He stopped throwing up and seemed to feel much better. That night as I tucked him into bed, Dr. John's words played on a loop in my head: "catastrophic death . . . catastrophic death." I begged, *"Please, Lord, don't let Todd's death be scary. If and when he dies, please let him be peaceful."* Later that night, when the house was dark and quiet, I went into Todd's room. I put my finger under his nose just to see if he was still breathing. I was relieved to feel the warm air on my finger. With great relief, I tiptoed back into my room and fell asleep.

On Sunday, remarkably, Todd wanted to go to church. Although he was weak, he actually felt pretty good. Pastor Danny planned to make an announcement to the congregation about Todd's condition and request a special time of prayer for him. I told Todd what was going to take place in the service, and he seemed fine with the idea. Our family sat in the overflow room of the church so that the large crowd in the sanctuary would not overwhelm him. As we watched the service on the projector screen, Pastor Brooks asked the church family to take a few minutes to pray for Todd in groups of two or three. Even in the overflow room I could hear Todd's name being spoken in prayer all around me. Hearing the prayers of people around me provided me with comfort and hope. I know Todd felt honored to know so many people were praying for him. After church, we ate lunch with some of our dearest friends, Trey, Shawn, and their children. We've been close for years; so close that we call ourselves the MacLurtey family, a combination of their last name—MacDonald—and ours. Trey and Shawn's four children are right about the same ages as our four. We have shared many fun times over the years, eating, traveling, and attending special events together. They have been a constant presence and comfort to our family.

At this meal, all the kids gathered at one end of the table, chatting and laughing. To my amazement, Todd ate a burger. He had barely eaten for months, but now that he was out of the hospital, he wanted a burger! It did my soul a world of good to see Todd laughing and enjoying food. As we ate, Trey looked at me and said, "We all need to go somewhere and make some memories. Where do you want to go?"

"Don't tempt me," I answered lowering my head. "I would love to go somewhere."

"I'm completely serious. Let's do it." I looked into his eyes and knew he meant it.

Immediately, my heart was all in, but realistically it didn't seem feasible. Shawn and David are both teachers, and all our kids were in school. Leaving right in the middle of the school year was no easy task. We had big hurdles to get over, but for every objection, Trey wisely reminded us that we had nothing more important to do than make memories with Todd.

After lunch, we headed over to the MacDonald's home, where the adults retreated to Trey's office to make the arrangements. The kids stayed together in another room, unaware of the scheming taking place a few feet away. Trey worked fast. We had met for lunch at noon, and by 3:00 we had twelve plane tickets and plans for five days in Orlando. After we settled job issues, got approval for the school absences, and finalized the tickets and accommodations, we ventured into the MacDonalds' family room to surprise the kids with the news that we were headed on a "MacLurtey" family trip to Florida the next day. The screams from all eight kids nearly deafened us; we almost wanted to join in and scream with them. We were going to have some fun and make some memories. Cancer would have to wait.

We started the day with our pastor telling the congregation that Todd probably would not make it. We ended the day with shouts of joy and laughter, thinking about the amazing week we would have together. As friends learned of our plans, we received an outpouring of their love. By the end of the night, we had a $200.00 check for spending money along with bags of snacks and bottled water for the trip. Everyone wished us well and assured us of their prayers that Todd would do well and our trip would be memorable.

Brenda Lurtey

Chapter 18

MacLurtey Family Trip

The next morning, Todd felt sick to his stomach. Worried, I watched as he threw up huge amounts of green bile. I prayed desperately, *"Lord, please give us this week together!"* After Todd vomited, he felt better and decided to visit his grandmother next door. I was grateful they could have some time together, but when he came home, he started feeling nauseated again. I wondered whether he could even make the trip. Still, we kept packing.

Finally, we were ready. As we started to pull out of the driveway, Amy called from the hospital. David stopped the car and I climbed out to speak with her privately. Gently, she asked, "Brenda, when do you want to call in hospice?" I had forgotten all about hospice!

"Believe it or not," I responded, "we are actually getting ready to fly to Florida for a family trip." The news surprised and pleased her. I promised to call her when we got back. Just then, I did not want to think about hospice or death.

After we arrived at the airport, we headed inside while David parked the car. Todd had just sat down in the lobby when he began throwing up in the garbage bag I had thought to bring with us. He threw up way more fluid than could possibly be in his stomach. Again, I begged, *"Please, Lord, give us this week together."*

After a few minutes Todd stood up and announced, "Wow, I feel so much better." Almost immediately, a huge change came over him. He seemed to have more energy, his smile returned, and, most surprisingly, he wanted food.

After we passed through security, all twelve of us waited by the departure gate. Todd sat next to me, happily sipping the sweet tea he had purchased earlier with money from David. As we waited for our flight, two police officers approached us. I looked at them, looked away, and looked back again. As they walked, they stared intently in our direction. I almost joked to Shawn that they were probably coming after Jeffrey and Buddy, our youngest partners-in-crime, but before I could get the words out, the officers reached us. One of them accused Todd, "You stole that sweet tea!"

My heart sank. In a split second, terrified thoughts ricocheted through my mind. *"Oh, my goodness, he is going to die in jail. Todd hasn't flown since he was an infant, so maybe he thought those beverage fridges along the walls were buffet style and everything was free. What if he really did steal? He's never done that before!"*

Confidently, Todd responded, "I didn't steal the tea. I have a receipt!"

I whipped my head over to look at him and thought, *"What kid keeps receipts? Thank you, Lord, that Todd kept his."*

The police officer took the paper from Todd's hand and asked us to come with him to the beverage station. He showed the clerk Todd's receipt. She giggled. "Oops. I thought he stole it."

The officer shook his head in disgust and turned to us. "I'm sorry about that. You're free to go."

Todd shrugged his shoulders and walked away, as if the entire horrifying encounter was no big deal. I was not so forgiving. I wanted to pounce on that woman like a mother bear. Thankfully, God shut my mouth, but as I walked away with the officer, I started to cry. "I can't believe she did that to my son. This is our last family trip together. He is dying of cancer."

The officer apologized profusely as he led me back to my seat. "I'm so sorry. She's mistakenly accused other people of stealing. I knew the minute I talked to your son that he was telling the truth."

The police officer walked away as Todd and I told the rest of the MacLurtey family what happened. A short time later, the officer came back and motioned for me to come over to him. He again apologized for the mistake, and promised me somehow he would make it up to us.

A short time later, he had arranged for Todd and me to get on the plane before the other passengers. Todd met the pilot and had his picture taken with him, and then we settled in our seats to wait for the other passengers. Before we took off, the airport manager boarded the plane and presented Todd with another sweet tea. The unexpected gift made Todd a happy young man. He loved his sweet tea. As the attendants ran through their safety check and greeted the passengers, one announced "A special welcome to Todd Lurtey on his first plane ride." All of us cheered and laughed. Shortly into the trip, the flight attendant gave Todd a free lunch box of food. The panic I felt when the police officers first approached us was horrible, but all the attention Todd got in the aftermath made up for it.

We settled into the flight, looking forward to the week ahead. Todd ate most of his boxed lunch, which surprised me, since he usually barely touched his food. Watching him, I thought in amazement, *"On Saturday we brought him home to die, and now we are on a plane headed for Florida."* Todd looked happy and almost energetic; an outsider would hardly know he was sick.

As we flew above the clouds, I looked out the window at the beautiful view spread out below us and thought, *"This must be what heaven looks like."* Tears sprang to my eyes and slowly rolled down my cheeks. I could not imagine life without Todd. Gratefully, I prayed, *"Thank you, Lord, that this isn't the day and this isn't the time."*

I loved watching Todd laugh and joke with the MacLurtey kids. He was clearly as excited as the rest of us to be going to Florida. After we landed in Orlando and rented a fifteen-passenger van, our first stop was at a beautiful beach. The trip from the van to the beach was a bit of a hike, especially for Todd. Up to this point, he had barely walked; we mostly took him from place to place in his wheelchair. He was extremely skinny and malnourished. As we walked, his legs kept giving out and that was hard to see. While the other kids explored the beach, I sat down on the sand and Todd leaned his back against my legs for support. The sun was setting as we looked out over the water. I don't know what was going through his mind, but I was trying to record that moment forever. I didn't know how much longer we had together, but I knew I always wanted to remember sitting with Todd, watching the waves and the sunset, wondering whether heaven looked anything like the picture before us.

Protectively, I wrapped my arms around him and tried to hold back my tears.

When it was time to eat, we walked a short distance along the sand to the beachfront restaurant. Our meal was wonderful, and it was so encouraging to hear the laughter and different conversations taking place among all twelve of us. After the meal, the adults sat around the table and continued to talk while the kids hung out on the beach, laughing and posing for pictures. Later, we drove about an hour and a half to our beautiful condominium. Todd was tired and ready to watch TV in bed for a while, but his broad smile told me he was happy. I was so thankful we could spend time with him in this wonderful place. I prayed we could just enjoy our time together and not think about going home to wait for Todd to die.

After a good night's sleep, we woke up refreshed and ready to take over Universal Studios. David rented a wheelchair for Todd so that he didn't have to walk all over the park. All the fun seemed to help Todd's appetite; he ate every time he had an opportunity.

While we were in Universal Studios, Dr. John called David to check on Todd's condition. Dr. John was shocked to hear David say, "Actually, we're at Universal Studios and Todd is doing great!" Thankfully, Todd had not thrown up once since we left the airport. He had more energy, but his legs still gave out when he tried to walk.

Remarkably, Todd wanted to go on all the rides, including upside-down roller coasters. Some of them obviously hurt his back, but he was not about to sit and watch everyone else have fun. Watching him, it was hard to fathom that just a few days ago we were discharged from the hospital so that he could die at home, and now I was watching him smile and laugh with dear friends as he went on park rides.

He didn't often share with me how he felt emotionally, but Shawn had a few moments to talk to him alone. Everyone was shopping in one of Universal Studios's stores and Todd was cold, so Shawn took him outside to sit in the sun.

Out of the blue, Todd said, "Mrs. MacDonald, do you think there will be roller coasters in heaven?"

Shawn was taken aback by Todd's question. Although she felt unqualified to give him an answer, she replied, "Todd, I don't know whether there will be roller coasters in heaven. We can probably fly, so we won't need roller coasters. Whatever is there will be way better than anything we have ever seen or could imagine."

When Shawn later told me about Todd's question, I experienced varying emotions. I felt peaceful and excited thinking about the wonderful things the Lord has prepared for us in heaven, and I felt some fear knowing that Todd was talking about heaven. I wanted death to be the farthest thing from his mind. With all my heart I wanted to believe the new tumor diagnosis was a mistake and that God was going to heal Todd.

While we were in Florida and shuttled from place to place in the van, I often watched Todd's reflection in the rearview mirror. As he looked out the window, I wondered what he was thinking. Was he scared? Did his question for Shawn about heaven mean he really understood he was dying? If so, what did that feel like to a fifteen-year-old kid? In reality, he was probably thinking, *"Why does my mother keep staring at me in the mirror? I wonder what's for supper."*

We had the time of our lives as the MacLurtey family. Trey and Shawn's oldest daughter, Katie, had twelve T-shirts printed with "MacLurtey" and all of our names on the back. We proudly wore those shirts as if we were one big, happy family. Although I tried to enjoy each moment, sometimes my emotions got the best of me and I wondered whether this was our last trip together. I could not bear the thought of losing Todd. When these thoughts crowded my mind, God gently reminded me not to borrow trouble from tomorrow. We still had Todd today!

We packed the four days we spent in Florida with fun, laughter, and priceless memories. Toward the end of the week, I began praying, *"Lord, is there anything else I can do for Todd? Are there any other options for treatment? If there is anything I can do, please guide me."* Almost immediately I thought about St. Jude Children's Hospital and Massachusetts General in Boston. I could hardly wait to get home and contact them both.

Before we left for Florida, I thought I would cry the whole way home, just knowing we were waiting for Todd to die. I did not feel that way anymore. I had something that I had not had for a long time. I had hope.

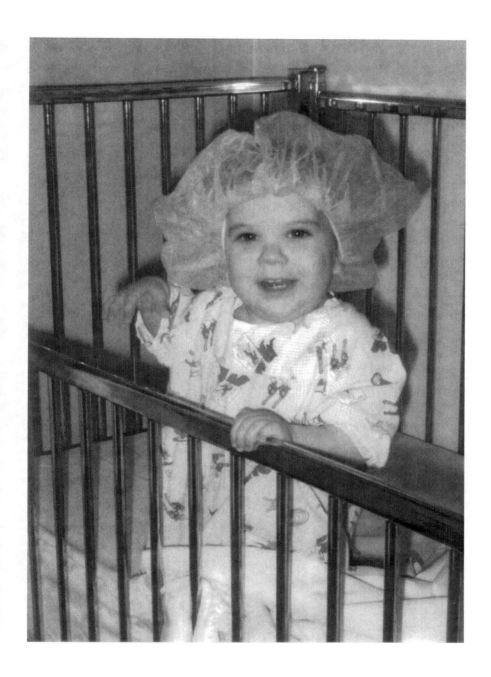

Todd's very first surgery

Todd was always such a happy child

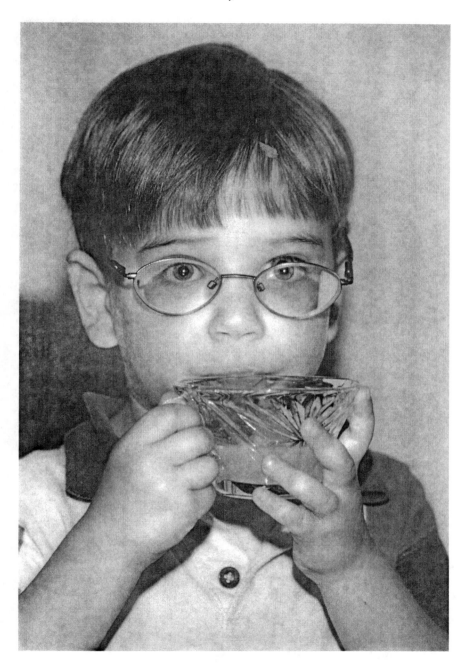

Todd at Uncle Bo's remission party

**Todd's first day of 9th grade
pictured with Brandon, Lauren and Jeffrey**

Extended family trip to Disney

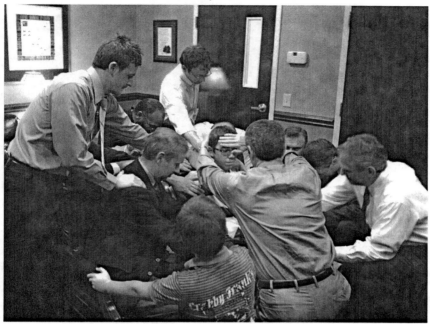

Our church elders prayed over Todd a few days before his biopsy

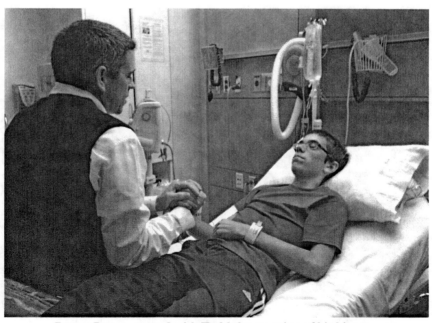

Pastor Danny prayed with Todd the morning of his biopsy

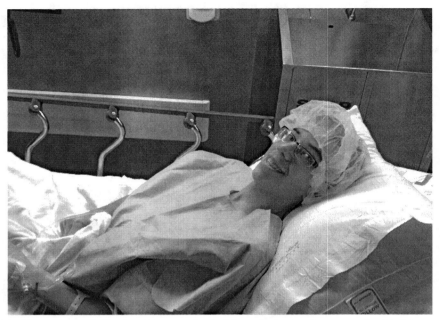

Todd was peaceful before he was wheeled into the operating room for his biopsy

Todd with "Uncle Bunny" after his tumor resection in Charleston

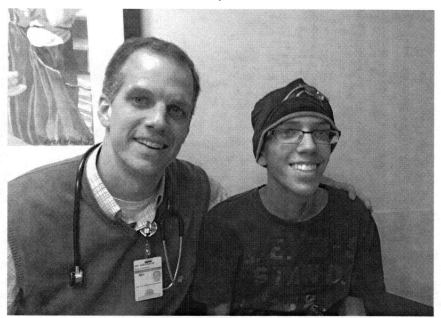

Todd and Dr. Alan—his first oncologist

Todd and Gracie

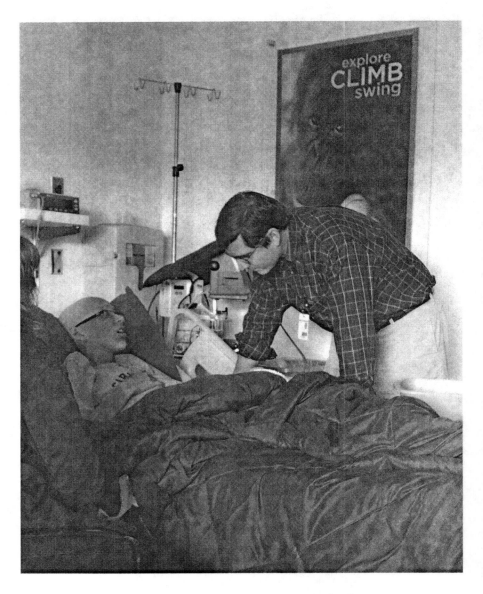

**A sweet interaction between Dr. John and Todd immediately
following our meeting in the "bad news room"**

Todd's smile—evidence of God's grace the day we left the hospital because nothing more could be done for him

"MacLurtey" family at Disney—a trip of precious memories

Todd, Cousin Quinn, and Uncle Andy on local television station to promote Late Skate fundraiser

Todd and Aunt Corinne at the fundraiser

Todd and his fabulous birthday cake made by my friend Sharon

The Lurteys meet Dolly Parton

I loved seeing all four of my children together

So grateful for treasured pictures taken of our family

Todd's first limo ride on his Wish Trip to NYC

**Thanks to the kindness of Lisa Valastro we made
lasting memories at Carlo's Bakery**

Todd was excited to meet "Cousin Anthony"

Our family at Carlo's Bakery in Lackawanna

We were so honored to meet Kelly Ripa and Michael Strahan

Todd with Dr. John and his sweet wife India

Mother's Day 2013— just two days after Todd passed away

Saying my final goodbye to my precious son

In my mind this is how I will always picture Todd in Heaven

Brenda Lurtey

Chapter 19

Renewed Hope

When our family arrived home from Florida, the Lord provided many events and tasks to occupy our time. I began contacting people at Mass General and St. Jude. I wanted to depart immediately for one of the two hospitals, but in the medical world, things rarely happen quickly. We had to talk with medical personnel, send scans, and wait for a week or two for panels of doctors to meet and discuss Todd's case. Frantically, I thought to myself, *"What in the world are we waiting for? Just get Todd up there and start some sort of treatment!"* Todd's case was of utmost importance to me, but no one else seemed to be in a hurry to help him.

On February 19, Pastor Danny invited us to bring Todd over to the church for a time of prayer. Our church was hosting a large group of pastors for a few days of meetings. The pastors wanted to lay hands on Todd and pray for him again. What a wonderful time of encouragement that was for David, Todd, and me. We didn't know all the men, but we appreciated their desire to pray for Todd. Pastor Danny and his son Luke joined them in the room. Luke faithfully prayed for Todd, and at times, he fasted while he prayed. Todd's youth minister, Pastor Abe, was there, as well as Pastor Matthew, one of our former pastors (and a lymphoma survivor) now serving God in New York. I felt certain, if for some reason God did not hear my prayers, He would surely hear the prayers of those godly pastors.

While we were in Florida, my brother-in-law, Andy, called David with an idea our niece Quinn had for a fundraiser to help us with our expenses. Now that we hoped to go out of town for more treatment, we needed additional funds. We enthusiastically supported her idea of a skate night fundraiser on March 2. To promote it, Quinn and Andy arranged to speak on a local television station about the event. Todd and I wanted to watch the interview, so we went with them to the station. After Todd met with the station manager, the crew thought he should be on the show with Quinn. They gave him a microphone and led him to the set. The hosts, Jack and Kimberly, asked Quinn to explain the purpose for the skate night. Quinn explained the burden the Lord had placed on her heart to help her cousin and his family with their mounting medical bills and then described the details of the upcoming skate night fundraiser.

Kimberly then turned her attention to Todd. "We want to learn more about your story because God has given you a struggle that fortunately not everyone has, but you are in a battle quite literally for your life."

"It's been wonderful. God has taught me so much. I've been battling cancer since September and it's just been wonderful. God is teaching me so much."

I could tell by the expressions on the faces of the show's hosts that his response was not what they expected to hear. It was not what I expected to hear. Because he was a little nervous about being on live TV and had had no time to prepare his comments, what he said came from his heart. I knew he wasn't saying that having cancer was wonderful but that what the Lord was in the process of teaching him was wonderful.

Jack asked Todd what kind of cancer he had. Todd explained that he was born with neurofibromatosis and that he had a malignant peripheral nerve sheath tumor. The tumor had recently been removed, but it was back, and he was hoping to go to Boston for further treatment.

Jack then asked Todd how he was feeling now. "I am feeling wonderful. I had feeding tubes in me, and they took those out and I am just doing a lot better."

Kimberly concluded her part of the interview. "Your attitude is unheard of because . . . there have to be times . . . you say it's wonderful, but being a human being, there have to be times where it was not so physically wonderful, and yet you've kept that attitude up and you're to be commended for that."

Andy added a few comments about the skate night and then Jack urged viewers to go out to the fundraiser and give so that Todd could get the treatment he needed. At one point in the interview he had asked Todd how old he was. Todd replied that he was 15, but about to be 16 in just a few days. Jack ended the interview by wishing Todd a happy birthday . . .

and many more. How I hoped and prayed that would be true for him. I left the interview excited and hopeful about what might come from it.

When the night of the fundraiser arrived, we had no idea how many blessings the Lord had in store for our family. We got to the ice skating rink early, where many people were busily setting up for the event. Quinn handed David, Todd, and me fluorescent orange T-shirts with the "thumbs down" symbol. The shirt read simply, "Dislike Cancer." We wore them proudly since we were in complete agreement with the sentiment. We definitely disliked cancer. Everywhere we turned, friends and even strangers greeted us with enthusiastic smiles and hugs, and before we knew it, the doors opened and people poured inside. We spent the entire evening surrounded by people who were there for one purpose: to support our family.

The fundraiser committee, made up of family members and friends, had one thousand bright orange bracelets made that read, "Praying for Todd Lurtey." By the end of the evening, fewer than one hundred bracelets remained. We really had no way of knowing how many attended the event, since it is possible that not everyone took a bracelet. We later learned that some people did not even make it to the skating rink because of the traffic jam Todd's supporters created.

Quinn picked out the food for the evening. Todd loved bacon and donuts, so that is what she wanted to serve. We also enjoyed homemade goods like cookies and chocolate-dipped pretzels. In one corner of the rink, guests posed for pictures at a photo booth. Later, the pictures were placed in an album for our family.

Todd had the time of his life. I could tell, because his smile never left his face. People crowded the building, talking, playing volleyball, and skating. I heard laughter and conversation everywhere I went. Todd was not strong enough to get out on the ice alone, so some of the skating instructors helped him "skate" around the rink with Quinn in a sled. Throughout the evening, hundreds of people hugged us and assured us of their continuing prayers for Todd and our family. We left the rink in the early hours of the morning physically exhausted but with a renewed inner strength and gratitude for all the friends, both old and new, who surrounded our family with prayer and lots of love.

Brenda Lurtey

Chapter 20

Looking for a Cure

Todd turned sixteen on March 4, 2013. For me, the day was bittersweet. While I was indescribably thankful that I had Todd in my life for those sixteen years, I couldn't help wondering whether this was his last birthday. Because our birthdays are back-to-back, we often took our birthday picture together. What would my future birthdays be like without him? Taking care of Todd and planning what I could do to help him consumed my life. I could not bear the thought of planning a party— even though this birthday needed to be celebrated more than any other. Fortunately, sweet friends of mine asked whether they could throw a party for Todd and invite the entire ninth grade. I loved the idea and was relieved to have this burden taken off my shoulders.

The afternoon of the party, after telling Todd I had a surprise for him, I blindfolded him, drove him to his school, and led him to the spot where his entire class waited to greet him. I struggled to hold back my tears when I removed his blindfold. A broad smile instantly covered Todd's face as all his friends began to sing "Happy Birthday" to him. The large cake, balloons, snacks, and cards obviously thrilled Todd, but more importantly, he was excited to be with his friends. He missed them.

My heart ached for Todd; so much had changed for him since his diagnosis. In a short time, he went from a carefree teen spending time with his friends, playing sports, and having fun, to staying with his mom all day, sapped of his strength, and probably dying of cancer. Despite all that, he never once complained that he had cancer. I knew it saddened him at times, but he mostly kept his feelings to himself. Throughout his illness, he never made me feel that he did not care to have me around. In fact, more than ever, he seemed to want me near him; my presence comforted him.

Later that evening, a special cake arrived at our house. Sharon, my college roommate and nurse for Todd's birth, had asked me a week or so earlier whether she could make Todd's birthday cake. Sharon makes amazing cakes, and this one was no exception. She has known Todd his whole life, and her creation showcased some of Todd's favorite things. One side of the cake replicated the Carolina Panther's Stadium—because the Panthers were Todd's favorite football team. The Dollywood sign, complete with butterflies, and a roller coaster covered another section of the cake. Fondant and chocolate sculptures of a glass of sweet tea, a piece of steak wrapped with bacon, a bowl of mashed potatoes with gravy, and a bowl of chocolate ice cream sat in front of the cake. The whole thing looked amazing and tasted great. Todd's face lit up the moment he saw it. As he checked out the individual elements, he kept repeating, "Wow, this is awesome!" I was so happy to see the joy on Todd's face that Sharon's gift brought to him, and I was blessed by her labor of love on behalf of Todd.

Brandon, Lauren, and Jeffrey still had a few weeks left of school. Every morning, after they left for the day, Todd and I sat together and we often watched *Live! with Kelly and Michael Show* or *Andy Griffith*. All the while, I would think, plan, and strategize about what I could do to help Todd. One day a friend called and suggested we visit a nutritionist. We had nothing to lose at this point, so I made an appointment. On March 6, Todd and I drove thirty minutes to meet Dr. Campbell. He told Todd that only God could truly heal, but he would use God's whole foods in their most natural state to help Todd's body. I appreciated that Dr. Campbell gave God the glory for any healing that would take place.

During our appointment, Dr. Campbell described a natural product made of fermented soy that has helped cure many different types of cancer. The beverage was extremely expensive; each eight-ounce bottle cost $50, and Todd was to drink a bottle a day. Normally, this would have been cost prohibitive for us, but funds raised from the skate night allowed me to order the product. I bought natural grape flavoring to add to the soy drink, because Dr. Campbell warned me it was tough to drink without flavoring. I also selected a chocolate protein powder to make healthy drinks for Todd. Cancer cannot live in an alkaline environment, so Dr.

Campbell provided a list of foods that are completely alkaline, those that are partially alkaline, and those that are not alkaline at all. I quickly realized most of the foods our family eats were on the non-alkaline list. I knew we were in for some trouble as I transitioned from our normal diet, but I was willing to do whatever it took to help Todd. The nutritional route seemed like the one to take, and I was eager to let the healing begin.

Unfortunately, Dr. Campbell had also explained that sugar would feed Todd's tumor, so sweet tea would have to go. The news upset Todd. He loved and craved his sweet tea; it was really one of the few things that tasted good to him anymore. I didn't want to deprive Todd of something he enjoyed, but I was determined to follow the nutritionist's guidelines. That night, at the referral of Dr. Campbell, I telephoned the man who invented the fermented soy product. He was kind, gracious, and willing to explain the theory behind his fermented soy product. After our conversation, I was convinced that Todd should try his product.

A few days after our trip to the nutritionist, Marilyn, my mother's cousin, came in from Canada for a visit. A retired nurse, she had dealt with many end-of-life patients. She came to do anything possible to help with Todd. I told her about the fermented soy product and our plan to try the alkaline diet. She read the material and agreed it sounded plausible. I could not be completely strict with the diet because Todd had to eat as much as possible. He did not have a feeding tube anymore, so we had to rely on his own appetite—which was little—to get his nutrition. Finally, the fermented soy beverage—in my mind, the answer to Todd's problems—came on the UPS truck. I was confident the $50-a-bottle drink would begin the healing process.

Marilyn did not want to make Todd try anything we hadn't tried ourselves, so she opened up a bottle and poured out a teaspoon. I always smell everything before I eat or drink it and when I smelled the liquid, I nearly threw up. It was awful! Still, I would drink a glass of pond scum to help Todd, so I plugged my nose and forced it down. Then it was Todd's turn.

"Todd, plug your nose and only breathe through your mouth until you finish the entire bottle. If you drink it this way, you won't taste the drink at all."

He took one sip and immediately threw up in the sink. My hopes were dashed. "Please keep trying, Todd!" I begged. Todd adamantly refused, repeating over and over, "I can't!"

I was so thankful Marilyn was with me. She saw my disappointment, but she also understood how difficult swallowing the horrible-tasting beverage was for Todd. She encouraged me to focus on the alkaline diet. The case of drinks cost over $1,000, so I called Dr. Campbell and described what happened. Marilyn and I took the case back to him the next day, and he graciously refunded my money—minus the cost of the bottle we opened—and suggested we try other options. We sampled another fermented soy product that tasted like Tang when added to orange juice. It was much more palatable than the other soy drink. In addition, he told me to give Todd one teaspoon of baking soda added to 3 teaspoons of pure maple syrup, a concoction that puts alkaline right into the bloodstream. The new options sounded promising and doable.

Every morning, I gave Todd a chocolate protein milkshake with a tablespoon of the maple syrup mix and some pure orange juice with the orange supplement powder. Todd saw right through my attempts to hide the nutritional supplements in his tried and true favorite drinks, but at first, he made a valiant effort to force them down. When he balked, I begged him to finish the drinks. In response, he promised, "Mom, I'm trying!" Getting him to consume the concoctions became a protracted battle, one I was losing. Marilyn could see my emotional struggle, and she tried to encourage Todd and me to stick with the plan. She also helped me put together our alkaline meals.

One weekend during Marilyn's visit, David and I took a two-day mini vacation. We needed time away from all the stress. I knew my kids would have fun with Marilyn, and she was fully capable of taking care of Todd. David and I appreciated the time alone together, but it was hard to relax. I had not been away from Todd in months. I missed him and just wanted to get back home to him.

All too soon, Marilyn had to return to Canada. We were all sad to see her leave. I am sure she knew she would not see Todd again in this lifetime, but I tried to hold out hope that the Lord might still heal him. My heart ached when she hugged Todd goodbye, especially when I heard him quietly say to her, "What do I do now?"

She lovingly replied, "Make memories, and I'll pray for you everyday."

After Marilyn left, I persisted in encouraging Todd to take the supplements, and we continued going to the cancer clinic for checkups.

The Lord gave us a period of respite between the time we went to Florida through Todd's birthday. I remember going to the cancer clinic the day after Todd's birthday. The report from that visit stated, "Remarkably, Todd is feeling well. He has been eating well. He is at least maintaining his weight. He is on no medications. He has no pain." The CT scan from that visit even showed that the tumor had stayed about the same size it had been in February. I was amazed, and I believed God had His hand on Todd's tumor to prevent it from rapid growth. Earlier in February, we had withdrawn Todd from school, but I began to wonder whether he should be reenrolled—I saw that much improvement in his condition.

The period of respite was brief. Eventually, St. Jude and Mass General notified us that there was nothing they could do for Todd that his Greenville oncologists had not already tried. I was unprepared for that response, and the news devastated me. Panicked, I gave a fleeting thought to taking Todd to Mexico. David and I had heard about people going to Mexico for alternative treatments, but I did not have any contacts there and did not know where to turn for help. I felt as though I was standing in an arena full of doctors, begging someone to step forward and help, but no one would. In desperation, I begged the Lord to give me direction. I saw Todd's condition begin to decline again, and I felt as if we were running out of time.

Todd and I usually got along great, but one day I got angry with him. I always watched him intently to make sure he finished the doctored orange juice and chocolate milk. One morning, he just would not—or could not—do it. I was furious. I had to leave the house to calm myself down. How could he not do his part to get better? I was frantically trying anything and everything to save his life. All he had to do was eat or drink what I put in front of him, but he would not. He knew I was mad at him when I left.

When I calmed down enough to come home, Todd met me at the door with tears in his eyes. "Mom, can I talk to you in your room?"

We sat on my bed, and he began to cry. Todd rarely cried, so his tears got my immediate attention. He said softly, "Mom, I'm sorry I'm a bad son. I am trying to eat the food and drink those drinks you give me, but they make me feel so bad. You just don't know how I feel inside."

My anger was immediately replaced with compassion, and I started crying too. Suddenly, I realized I was not mad at Todd; my anger was just a reaction to the great fear I felt inside. I gathered him in my arms and held on for dear life. "Todd, you aren't a bad son at all! You're a wonderful son, and I love you. You're my hero! You have been through more in sixteen years of life than I have been through in all of mine. I'm so sorry, Todd. I know you are doing your best. God understands exactly how you feel inside, even when the rest of us don't have a clue how you feel."

Todd leaned against me as I told him how much I loved him, and how proud I was of him. I promised him I would stop pressuring him. I had explained how I thought the doctors could heal him, the medicine would heal him, the supplements would heal him, but in that moment, my heart changed. I knew our eyes had to be completely on God. If Todd were going to be healed, the miracle would come only from God. We were not going to rely on any more crutches. Everything was in God's hands. I no longer had any plans of my own for Todd's healing. I truly believed that God could—and maybe would—heal Todd just to prove the healing came from God alone. I no longer felt like I was fighting for Todd's life. I was trusting God for Todd's life.

Every night I tucked Todd into bed before he went to sleep, and every night I walked out of his room with tears running down my cheeks. I tried to have an attitude of trust, but if my time with Todd was slipping away, I wanted to remember every single moment.

Chapter 21

Dollywood

Toward the beginning of Todd's illness, Brandon contacted a Dollywood representative asking whether Dolly could send Todd a letter of encouragement. He described Todd's battle with cancer and explained that Todd was a big fan of Dollywood. A few weeks later, Todd received an autographed picture from Dolly that read, "To Todd, Get Well Soon. Love, Dolly." Todd was beyond thrilled, which made us happy. Weeks later, a Dollywood representative contacted us and asked whether we would like to meet Dolly at the park. We didn't need to give it a second thought. We were thrilled for this opportunity. We told Todd we were going to Dollywood but let meeting Dolly be a surprise.

We headed to Pigeon Forge on March 22, where we stayed in a cabin with my sister and her family. The night before our special meeting, we let Todd in on the big secret. We were so excited to meet Dolly that it was hard to sleep that night. The next morning we got up early and drove to the park. Dollywood was not even open yet, but two representatives met us at the entrance, led us through some back doors, and left us in Dolly Parton's personal dressing room! We waited about fifteen minutes before we heard that country accent call out, with two syllables instead of one, "TO-OD? Where's Todd Lurtey?"

As Dolly walked in, Todd broke out into his famous grin. Dolly was as nice as she could be. She hugged all of us, posed for several pictures, and autographed a photo for each of us. At the end of our meeting, she had one picture left. She asked whether we could think of anyone to give it to. We thought for one second before deciding it had to go to Kristen.

Laughing, I told Dolly about a mean trick Kristen and I played on Todd when he was just a little boy. Kristen and I knew how much Todd loved Dollywood. Unfortunately, he was also very gullible. As a joke, I asked Kristen to call Todd and pretend to be Dolly Parton. We had just returned from a family trip to Dollywood, so the timing was perfect. I made sure Todd answered the phone and then watched his face as he talked. Kristen asked, in her best "Dolly" voice, "Is this the Lurtey residence?"

Todd answered, "Yes."

"This is Dolly Parton." At that news, Todd's eyes grew big as saucers. Kristen went on. "Have you ever been to Dollywood?"

Todd yelled excitedly, "Yes, we were just there. We love your park!"

As Kristen continued to ask questions in her fake "Dolly" accent, I could see the thrill on his face and hear the excitement in his voice. Finally, Kristen told him who she really was. Todd's face dropped. He was crushed. Sadly, he finished the conversation with Kristen and hung up the phone. I tried to console him. "Todd, I'm so sorry. We were just playing a joke."

Todd wasn't mad at us; he was just extremely disappointed, and I felt awful. The next time Kristen saw Todd, she apologized for her part in the prank, and he graciously forgave both of us. Later we all laughed about the joke, but neither one of us ever forgot Todd's disappointment.

After I relayed the story to Dolly, she took great pity on Todd and jokingly yelled out, "That's terrible!" She wrote on Kristen's picture, "Dear Kristen, No more tricks! I love Todd. Love, Dolly Parton." Dolly had vindicated Todd after all these years. Kristen laughed when Todd later gave her the picture, and I think she will always treasure that gift.

After meeting Dolly, we visited some attractions, but Todd did not feel up to participating. Brandon, Lauren, and Jeffrey yelled and laughed as they rode the roller coasters. I observed Todd watching them from his wheelchair, and my heart ached for him. He always loved going on all the rides, but now his body was too weak and he was in too much pain to enjoy them. I wondered what he was thinking, but he just sat quietly, and I didn't know what to say to make him feel better.

Later, we used the meal vouchers the park provided to eat in one of Dolly's restaurants. Todd didn't have much of an appetite. I felt sorry for him, because under normal circumstances, he would have taken full advantage of the buffet. That afternoon, from front row seats, we watched a show in which Dolly made an appearance. Our last view of her was in a parade toward the end of the day. Dolly caught a glimpse of Brandon and gave him a special wave. The day was wonderful, and meeting Dolly was a great thrill, but I spent most of the day studying Todd and wishing I could take away his pain.

Brenda Lurtey

Chapter 22

Goodbyes

When we had first arrived at the hospital in October, Jaimie, the child life specialist at the cancer clinic, told us that Todd would get to "Make a Wish." Typically, so that they can actually enjoy the trip, the Make a Wish Foundation grants kids their wish after they complete their treatments. At the time, we knew we had a while before Todd finished his, so Todd and I talked about different options. Todd suggested attending a Panther's game. His dad and I could afford to take the family to a game, so I encouraged him to pick something else—something we could never do for him.

As time went on and because Todd's illness caused so many complications, I began to worry that he would never experience a "wish." Several times, the oncologists reminded me to turn in his form, but Todd and I never finalized his plans. When we took him home to live out his final days, I gave up on the idea. But during one of our last clinic visits, Jaimie told me that Children's Wish Foundation International could rush his request. Todd and I again discussed different ideas before I filled out the form in as much detail as possible. Within a few days, someone from the Foundation called to firm up dates and the specifics of Todd's wish. Todd wanted to go to New York City and stay at The Plaza Hotel where *Home Alone 2* was filmed. We scheduled the trip for a Mother's Day departure. I prayed Todd would make it.

On April 8 I took Todd to the cancer clinic. He didn't want to eat, his shoulder hurt, and he was extremely tired. Dr. Nichole determined that he needed some fluids. After receiving IV fluids for a few hours, I noticed quite an improvement in Todd. I was thankful for the fluids and grateful once again for the wonderful care given by Todd's oncologists. Three days later, Todd and I returned to the cancer clinic. He told Dr. Rebecca that he was having shortness of breath just walking from his bedroom out to the family room. He could also feel his heart racing. An x-ray revealed fluid collecting in his right lung and some concerning heart issues. I asked Dr. Rebecca if she and I could speak privately for a few minutes. I told her everything we had tried to help Todd, including the fact that we considered going to Mexico. Although she listened compassionately, there was nothing she could do for Todd except to help make him comfortable. She and I both believed Todd was getting worse. I knew it was time to make serious plans to set up hospice care. Before going back into Todd's room, she offered me a comforting hug.

One week later, Todd and I went to the cancer clinic for a scheduled appointment. I was glad to go. I noticed Todd's stomach was really protruding in the front and the side, a sign that seemed to indicate that fluid was collecting in his abdomen again. I wanted to see whether the doctor could drain his stomach to give him some relief. Instead, he sent Todd for an x-ray. When Dr. Alan came in to discuss the results, he told me there really was not much fluid in his abdomen; the tumor was growing. My heart sank. I could not imagine the size of the tumor. I left the room so Todd would not see my tears. I had struggled so hard to be brave. I tried everything I could to save Todd's life, but nothing I did was good enough. God had seemingly given me His answer. His will was not to heal Todd in this lifetime; God's will was to take him home to heaven. Todd was going to die, probably in just a short matter of time.

I told Dr. Alan about exploring nutritional solutions and cutting out Todd's sweet tea. With characteristic compassion, he told me eliminating sweet tea was not going to save Todd's life. Without him having to say it, I knew the truth. Nothing was going to save Todd. We had seemingly exhausted all of our resources.

Dr. Alan continued talking about the tumor, but I zoned out. A mother's heart can take only so much. The truthful words he spoke were too painful to absorb. When I stepped back into the clinic room, Todd asked me what Dr. Alan and I had talked about. Candidly, I explained, "Todd, you don't have fluid in your stomach. The tumor is growing."

He looked disappointed and searched my eyes to see my reaction to the news. Although my tears again welled up, I reminded him, "Todd, our times are in God's hands; your life on this earth was always going to be from March 4, 1997, until whenever God calls you home. Cancer will not shorten your life, so we don't need to worry." Although he didn't say anything, his face no longer showed disappointment, and this composed reaction showed me that he agreed with my words. I smiled and added, "Todd, the doctor said it's okay for you to drink some sweet tea." A smile lit up his face. He seemed so happy; you would have thought I had just offered him the moon.

Before we left the clinic, I glanced into a room where kids go if they are just receiving fluids or a daily chemo. Taniesha's mom, Marilyn, was sitting beside the bed where Taniesha was sleeping. I hadn't seen Taniesha for several months, so I eagerly rushed in to see her. I quietly gave Marilyn the news we had just received. She immediately wrapped me in her arms. I knew her heart hurt for me. We mothers on the cancer floor understood each other's pain, and that shared understanding bonded our hearts together. Looking at Taniesha, I remembered her kindness to Todd the day they first met. I hoped and prayed she would survive. At this point, she was in remission; she was at the clinic because she needed some fluids. Although I asked Marilyn not to awaken her, she insisted Taniesha would want to see us. A few moments later, Todd joined me in the room as Taniesha opened her sleepy eyes. As soon as she saw us, her beautiful smile spread across her face. Todd responded with a broad smile of his own. We spent a few sweet moments together. When it was time for us to leave, Marilyn gave Todd and me a hug goodbye. I don't know whether at the time Marilyn suspected she would not see Todd again in this lifetime. I certainly did not know it was the last time I would ever see Taniesha (her cancer returned a short time later and she went to be with her Savior six months after Todd died.) We left the clinic that day not knowing it was the last time any of the oncologists would see Todd.

We stopped for sweet tea as soon as we left the hospital. Grinning, Todd savored the taste he had missed for so long. His enjoyment over such a simple pleasure in the face of our devastating news brought fresh tears to my eyes.

As soon as we returned home from the cancer clinic appointment, I called the representative at the Children's Wish Foundation to let them know Todd might not make it to Mother's Day. Rather than cancel the trip, she suggested going that weekend. I didn't think David would be able to take more time out of his teaching schedule or that that kids could miss any more school, but I was wrong. David's boss and coworkers all told him to go on the trip, and they would cover his classes. The kids' principal graciously allowed them to take more days off from school. The Children's Wish Foundation representative called me the next day and told me she had everything in place for the trip and that the money to cover our expenses would be overnighted to us. All of the travel arrangements and packing was done at breakneck speed. We were scheduled to leave for Todd's Wish Trip at 7 a.m. on Friday, April 19. In my heart, I knew this was our last family trip together. I asked the Lord for grace to enjoy each day and strength not to think about the days to come. Matthew 6:34 was a powerful reminder of how important living in the moment was for me. "Therefore do not be anxious about tomorrow, for tomorrow will be anxious for itself." I also focused on 2 Corinthians 12:9: "My grace is sufficient for you, for my power is made perfect in weakness." I knew God gives us grace only for our present moments, not for our future. I clung to that promise.

Chapter 23

Wish Trip

At the airport, I warned Todd not to go anywhere near the woman who accused him of stealing the iced tea on our last trip. Fortunately, we left from a different terminal.

As we sat in the airport waiting for our departure, I thought about our other "MacLurtey" family members, and I wished they could join us on our trip. It was hard to get excited about the trip knowing the graveness of Todd's health. As we flew above the clouds, I thought of heaven and wondered about its beauty. What would it be like to finally meet Jesus face to face? Without a miracle, Todd would leave us shortly, and I couldn't imagine my life without him. I looked across the aisle at him and watched him as he slept—all the while praying that our time in NYC would be precious.

We arrived in NYC shortly after nine. An airport representative met us at our gate with a wheelchair and whisked us away down private corridors and elevators. Before we knew it, we were outside by the curb where the driver of a beautiful black SUV invited us to step inside. David sat up front with the driver and learned all about the landmarks we passed on our way to The Plaza Hotel. I knew about The Plaza from books and magazines, but I never dreamed we would stay there. White-gloved doormen opened the door for us, and we stepped into grandeur like we had never seen before. Five or six people greeted us in the lobby, introducing themselves and explaining what they would do for us that week. One gentleman even offered to unpack our clothes!

I am sure our eyes were as big as saucers as the staff escorted us to the sitting area of our suite. We were unaccustomed to such luxury; normally, we stay in hotels where the sitting area is the bed. The Plaza exceeded our wildest expectations. Chandeliers lit the sitting room and gold fixtures sparkled everywhere. Tiers of French macarons, chocolate-covered strawberries, candies, and cookies waited for us. Fresh roses brightened the room. David and I toured the master suite and bathroom where we found scented French soaps and fluffy bathrobes. Brandon and Todd had their own suite, complete with a huge bathroom. Lauren and Jeffrey stayed on the pullout couch in the fancy sitting room. Our accommodations were fabulous, and we were excited about all the fun ahead.

The trip coordinator gave us plenty of money for food, taxis, subways, and gifts. At lunchtime, we made our way to a nearby restaurant. Unfortunately, Todd was cold and his back hurt. I tried to navigate his wheelchair carefully on the bumpy sidewalks to make him as comfortable as possible. The restaurant served good food, but we had to wait for a bit. Jeffrey, worn out from the early morning, fell asleep at the table. The meal was expensive, so we were thankful for the money the Foundation provided. After lunch, we went back to the room so that Todd could rest. All of NYC lay before us, but we could not explore it because Todd was too tired. We all tried to be sensitive to him. This was his trip, and we wanted him to enjoy it.

Our first evening, we were supposed to take a limo to Bobby Flay's Mesa Grill restaurant for supper. Todd had looked forward to riding in a limo ever since he and I began talking about his Wish Trip. We waited outside for quite a while, but the limousine never came for us. The hotel staff tried to reach the driver. When they couldn't, they offered one of their fancy hotel vehicles at no charge to take us to the restaurant. Todd was visibly disappointed, but he didn't say anything. Bobby Flay wasn't in the restaurant that night, but the wait staff was wonderful, and the food was delicious. Our meals were slow getting to our table, though, and Todd was hungry, cold, and tired. One of our children spilled a drink all over the table. Again, Jeffrey fell asleep. We must have seemed so bumbly. By this time, it was about nine, and we had all been up since early morning. The whole restaurant buzzed with excitement, but none of us felt like talking.

Just before we headed back to the hotel, the wait staff surprised us with a special dessert for Todd. On a large sampler plate filled with desserts, they had written "Happy Birthday" in chocolate. When they presented the desserts, they sang "Happy Birthday" to Todd. This was the end of April and his birthday was in March, but we appreciated the kind gesture. Apparently, they did not realize the purpose of our trip.

After dinner, we learned the hotel driver was not coming to pick us up, so we had to take a taxi back to the hotel. I had never hailed a taxicab, much less ridden in one, so I had no clue what to do. One of the restaurant staffers graciously hailed the cab for us. We had to collapse Todd's wheelchair and get him situated before the cab driver took off. The trip back to The Plaza was quite an adventure. New York City cab drivers may know what they are doing, but we still had white knuckles when we arrived at our destination. David and I rode in separate cabs because our whole family could not fit in one. I was relieved to see his cab screech up behind mine.

We were pleasantly surprised to find someone had prepared our room with slippers by our beds and bottles of Fiji water on the bed stands. Our covers were folded down, and the side lamps were turned on. This pampering happened every single night! When we called our concierge for directions to the ice dispenser, he told David someone would bring our ice. Not long after, a gentleman with white gloves knocked on our door, delivering a silver bucket of ice. Now, that's what I call service!

Everyone was very tired after an early morning, so we all got into bed shortly after arriving back at The Plaza. As David and I lay discussing the events of the day, we found it humorous that we were actually staying at The Plaza Hotel! We were surrounded by luxury for the first time in our lives. How did it feel for people who were able to experience it all the time? As special as our accommodations were for us, what was most important to us was the fact that our whole family was still together. We prayed for strength for Todd and for wonderful memories to be made in the week ahead.

Brenda Lurtey

Chapter 24

Plans and Patience

Everyone slept pretty well that night, and we were excited for our first full day in New York City. We bounded out of bed, but Todd's physical condition made getting him up in the morning difficult. With Todd, nothing happened quickly any longer. Brandon, Lauren, and Jeffrey got impatient when Todd complained about loud noises or talking—loud sounds often frustrated him to tears. Although it was hard for Brandon to deal with Todd's new uncharacteristic emotions, I was thankful Brandon and Todd roomed together. Todd did not share his heart with Brandon as I hoped he would, but knowing Brandon was right there if Todd needed him comforted me, especially since my room was quite a distance from theirs.

We ate breakfast at a little place around the corner from our hotel, where they served coffee and all kinds of pastries. It was convenient and tasty, so we ate there each morning of the trip. Afterwards, we ventured into Times Square. I lived on Long Island as a child and often went through New York City, but I had never really experienced it. The city amazed me. I felt so small among such tall buildings.

Times Square teemed with people; for people watchers, it is the place to be. All of us looked around in amazement and snapped tons of pictures. We were especially excited when we saw ourselves on the Times Square jumbotron! As I walked along the streets, I saw all sorts of people from all walks of life. Some people were obviously well-to-do, while other people leaned against buildings asking whether we could spare some change. Although there were multiple sights to capture my attention, my thoughts often drifted back to Todd's sickness and heaven. How much longer would the Lord allow us to have Todd? What would it be like for him to go to heaven? I looked at life going on all around me and wondered how many of the people around us knew they would not take their riches to heaven. Did any of the poor people realize that there is a God in heaven who loves them and could provide for all their needs?

It was hard to keep my thoughts on the present and not worry about the future, but the Lord helped me. I wanted to make memories and not focus on sadness. Lauren and I ventured into a huge American Girl store, and David and the boys went into stores that interested them. After lunch at a two-story McDonalds, we visited FAO Swartz, the M&M Store, and any other stores that caught our attention. We wanted the kids to have a real New York experience, so we found a New York-style pizza place for supper. We did a lot of eating, but we also did a lot of walking! The rest of us were full of energy, but Todd could barely get in and out of his wheelchair. Each day, around suppertime, Todd's energy was spent, and he wanted to rest in the room—that was hard on Brandon, Lauren, and Jeffrey. We were in New York City, we had money to spend, but all we could do at night was sit in the room. We all battled with feelings of frustration from time to time. As a family, we are all used to coming and going quickly—we are all adventurous. However, things had changed. Our hurried lives had come to an abrupt halt. Todd had to be our main focus, and his needs and comfort had to be our top priority.

On Sunday, we got up early and took taxicabs to our friend's church in Manhattan. Pastor Matthew Hoskinson had served at our home church before he relocated to Manhattan to become the pastor of a church there. His familiar face was a welcome blessing, and we enjoyed seeing him in his new element. Matthew is a lymphoma survivor, so I hoped he could talk to Todd about how Todd felt emotionally. I still didn't know whether Todd knew he was dying or whether he was scared. I didn't want to ask Todd those questions myself because I didn't want to upset him, and I still held some hope that God would heal him. We wanted to stay for the church luncheon after the service so that Todd and Matthew could talk, but when I asked Todd whether he wanted to talk to Matthew privately, he responded, "No, I just want to go back to the hotel." I was disappointed but honored Todd's wishes. Before Matthew dropped us off at The Plaza, he gave Todd a voucher for a massage in the hotel spa and made plans to meet us on Tuesday. While Todd rested in his bed, David and I ventured to the basement mall of the hotel to check out our lunch options. We tried to find items we normally wouldn't eat at home.

At 1:30, a limo was scheduled to take us to the Broadway production *Wicked* at the Gershwin Theatre. I prayed this time it would actually show up. I knew Todd wanted to ride in a limo, but he kept being disappointed. Much to our delight, a beautiful, black stretch limo pulled up in front of us. We felt important climbing inside, especially since none of us had ever been in one before. People look at you differently when you step out of a stretch limo. You aren't just anybody—you are somebody! When we pulled up in front of the theater, people milled around, eagerly watching to see who would get out of the car. Much to our dismay, no one starting snapping photos of us once they realized we weren't celebrities.

Brandon was probably the most thrilled to see *Wicked*. He and I had seen it in Charleston; I liked it, but Brandon loved it! He couldn't wait to share the experience with Todd, and Todd seemed anxious to see what was so special about this production. Before the show began, we bought snacks and drinks in souvenir cups and then found our seats. Some people may get to do this type of thing all the time, but money is tight in our family. Normally we shared one or two drinks, but this time, we all bought what we wanted, and no one had to share. Todd smiled broadly. He appeared to enjoy himself despite his normal pain. The show was spectacular, and we were happy we could enjoy the experience together.

The limo picked us up again after the show was over. We had hoped to visit Central Park that night, but Todd needed to rest, so we went back to the hotel and settled him in his room. Brandon stayed to watch a movie with Todd while David and I took Lauren and Jeffrey to a nearby restaurant. Although we had a nice time at our dinner, I wished our whole family could be together. I didn't like the idea of our family being apart, even for a short time, because I knew it was only a matter of time before it would be our reality.

Brenda Lurtey

Chapter 25

A Dream Come True

On Monday we caught a ferry over to Hoboken, New Jersey, to visit Buddy Valastro's Carlo's Bakery. Buddy and his family appear on a few reality shows on The Learning Channel. Our family loves to watch *The Cake Boss* and *The Next Great Baker,* so the visit to Carlo's Bakery was one of the most exciting parts of the trip for all of us. We were not sure we would meet any of the Valastros, but we hoped we would. We had visited the bakery about two years earlier and had the pleasure of meeting some family members. Their baked goods are phenomenal, and we were excited to experience them once again. Todd seemed to have energy that day, and I was hopeful that he would enjoy the events of the day.

When we arrived at the bakery, we were escorted into a back room where we met Lisa Valastro, one of Buddy's sisters. Lisa offered us our favorite Carlo's Bakery treats, lobster tails—a crispy, delicious pastry filled with cream. It's a taste I will never forget! She also gave the kids Carlo's Bakery T-shirts. As the kids and I were indulging in our lobster tails, David privately told Lisa that Todd was on his Wish Trip because he was dying of cancer. She was filled with compassion and wanted to do all she could to give us a wonderful experience. Most of her family was working in the other bakery at Lackawanna, so Lisa arranged for us to meet some of them and even hailed cabs for our transportation. While we waited in the lobby for a tour of the Lackawanna bakery, Buddy's mother, Mary Valastro, arrived. Because of her physical difficulties she was in a wheelchair, just like Todd. I could tell she was vivacious and had a sweet and spunky personality. After we introduced ourselves, she asked me why Todd was in a wheelchair. I told her about his cancer and Wish Trip. In response, she said, "Oh, I want to hug him." As Todd moved closer to her, she gathered him in her arms. We talked to her for a few more minutes and she willingly posed for pictures with us before we toured the bakery.

After touring different parts of the bakery, we ended up in the main decorating room, which Todd and I, two die-hard *Next Great Baker* fans, found particularly thrilling. In no time, we met Grace Valastro, her husband, Joey, and Cousin Anthony. Todd especially wanted to meet Cousin Anthony since the pranks played on him were Todd's favorite part of the show. Anthony did not disappoint; he graciously took time to talk to Todd and even showed us another special room in the bakery. I was so happy for Todd as I watched his joyful interaction with Cousin Anthony.

Todd's next huge treat was meeting Ralph and Tyne, two of the sculptors. They were amazing, and we happily watched them work for over an hour. Fortunately, they did not seem annoyed with us. Instead, they answered our questions and gave us insight into what really goes on behind the scenes—funny stories and all. With the help of the decorators, Brandon, Todd, Lauren, and Jeffrey decorated their own cakes. None of the employees rushed us along to get back to their own work. They willingly gave of their time and interacted with the kids in a way that touched me. The Valastro family and their bakery employees are famous, and we were strangers to them. They had no reason to give us so much of their time except for the fact that their hearts were kind and compassionate. I am sure they didn't realize the young boy they made so happy wouldn't be on the earth much longer, but in their kindness, they unknowingly made cherished memories for a family that had very little time left together.

Before we boarded the ferry to return to the city, we met with a representative from the Children's Tumor Foundation, the organization that supports people with NF1. Todd presented the representative a check for a portion of the funds raised at the skate night. Unfortunately, our meeting was brief. We snapped a photo of the two of them and headed toward the ferry.

The thought of getting off the ferry and navigating our way through the subway carrying four cakes and pushing a wheelchair felt overwhelming. After David had a conversation with the ferry captain, he offered to get us on another boat that docked closer to The Plaza. Thanks to his kindness, we could take two boat rides and avoid the subway entirely. The second boat landed close to the Empire State Building. We had free passes, so we coaxed Todd up with us. We didn't stay long. The air was frigid, and Todd was worn out after the long day. I put a blanket over his head and face in an effort to warm him, but it didn't help much. I looked out over the vast city in amazement, yet it was hard to enjoy. I knew Todd was suffering, and I needed to get him inside the building for warmth.

On Tuesday, we spent a couple of pleasant hours eating lunch and shopping with Pastor Matthew. He helped us negotiate the subway and even wheeled Todd around. Later, we met up with another friend from our hometown. Rob also used to attend our church, but he's now a pastor in another part of New York City. We hung out with Rob in the basement mall before Todd got the massage Pastor Matthew had arranged for him at the hotel spa. Professional massages made wonderful gifts because Todd's back ached continually, and my puny massages didn't make him feel much better. We found out later that Todd's masseuse was the one always chosen for royalty staying at The Plaza. The Lord was so kind to choose the hands, normally reserved for royalty, to bring comfort to Todd.

Brenda Lurtey

Chapter 26

A Show and a Send-Off

We checked out of The Plaza on Wednesday morning. Our flight didn't leave until later, so we left our luggage in a secure area of the hotel and went to watch a taping of *Live! with Kelly and Michael*. Todd and I were especially delighted because we watched that show together many mornings after David left for work and the kids left for school. When we arrived at the studio, we gave our names to the woman with the clipboard just as we had been instructed to do. She brought us inside and escorted us to the VIP waiting area. As a special honor for Todd, we would enter the studio before the other audience members.

Before the show started, we filed into the studio and sat on the front row. The kids and I could not wait to see Kelly and Michael; David wanted to see all the television cameras and equipment. He teaches radio and television courses, so he was in a dream world of his own. The show is live, so the manager came in and explained to the audience what certain signals meant. Before long, the theme music started, and Kelly Ripa and Michael Strahan walked into the studio. They stood about two feet in front of us. Todd beamed with excitement, and all of us stood up, clapping and cheering. At the break, Kelly and Michael came over to meet us and invited us to spend time with them after the show.

Being part of live television was exciting for all of us. David was in his element looking at all the lights, cameras, and wires. Although Todd did not talk much, his wide smile and gleaming eyes told me he was having fun. When filming ended, we went backstage to visit with Kelly and Michael. They gave each of us hugs, posed for pictures with us, and made us feel genuinely welcome. They are celebrities, but they are also real, down-to-earth people. Nearly everyone asks me whether Kelly is as thin in person as she is on television. The answer is no. She is even thinner. When Kelly wanted to take a picture of the two of us side by side, I responded with laughter. "There is no way I'm standing beside you. We'd look like the number ten!" Instead, I pulled her in front of me, stuck my head beside hers, and someone snapped a picture. We had a wonderful time, and it warmed my heart to see the enjoyment on Todd's face.

After the taping, we took a cab to the Museum of Natural History. We hoped to see a lot of the scenery we saw in *Night at the Museum 2*, but we learned that not much of the movie was actually filmed there. After lunch, it was time to collect our things from the hotel and leave for the airport. Like all good things, our wonderful week had come to an end and my heart felt heavy.

When we arrived back at The Plaza, many of the staff members gathered in the lobby to give Todd a proper send-off. We shared lots of hugs and well wishes. Todd received a nice book signed by several Plaza employees, and our family got a box of cookies and a souvenir replica of the New York City skyline. A driver in a sleek black vehicle drove us to the airport and helped us unload our luggage at the curbside check-in. The driver left far too quickly. Once again, we were just ordinary people.

All of us were quiet and deep in thought as we made our way to the security checkpoint. I thought back over all the wonderful times we had had together the past week. *"What now, Lord? What now?"* We had nothing left to look forward to; the future seemed ominous.

Chapter 27

Delayed Departure

Airports handle people in wheelchairs very carefully—and quickly. I was surprised at how easy it was for me to take Todd through security. David and the other kids had to stand in line with the rest of the crowd. The doll Lauren bought in New York City received special scrutiny. The TSA agent inspected it carefully, put it through an x-ray machine, and wiped it down with a special cloth. I am not sure what they were looking for, but I wanted to chuck that doll by the time all was said and done!

Finally, we got to our gate with Todd, the wheelchair, and twelve carry-on items. Todd was tired, and we were all bummed about heading home. It was not long before we were informed that the airline had canceled our flight. If we could have run after that sleek black van to take us back to The Plaza Hotel, believe me, we would have caught it! Ordinarily we would have slept in the airport or made our own hotel arrangements, but when David explained our special circumstances, the airline arranged accommodations for us nearby. The four cakes the kids had made at Carlo's Bakery were among the twelve carry-on items, and we were not about to part with them. We left the airport with six suitcases, twelve carry-ons, and a wheelchair that we had to lug into a hotel van. Once we arrived at the hotel, we had to haul everything to our rooms. We tried to be thankful for the provision of the airport hotel, but it was a far cry from The Plaza Hotel! There were no slippers placed by our beds, and there was no fresh Fiji water on the side tables.

Early the next morning, we all hauled our luggage and twelve carry-ons back down to the hotel lobby and onto the shuttle. At the airport, we had to go through the whole security process again—and then there was that doll! We all had to wait while the doll was scrutinized and, again, put through a special security process. We finally made it through security and returned to our gate. The delay might have been a good thing; staying in the airport hotel and going through the security process made us appreciate going home.

The plane had two seats on one side and one seat on the other, which meant we couldn't all sit together. David and Todd were a few rows ahead of me. I sat next to a businessman, and the owner of the business sat across the aisle. As I talked with the men, I eventually told them about Todd, his cancer, and the Wish Trip. They asked lots of questions. During the flight, one of my children went to the back of the plane to use the restroom. Seconds later, I looked over and noticed that the company owner's drink had spilled all over his nice khaki pants. I hated to ask, but knew I had to. "Did my child bump you and spill your drink?" As I asked, I thought, *"Please don't say yes. Please don't say yes."*

Of course, "Yes" is exactly what he said. As I apologized, the man next to me started laughing, and then the company owner started laughing. Who was I to be left out? I joined them. His partner proclaimed how he could not wait to watch the owner give his presentation with spilled drink all over his pants. The victim took the mess well, but I think we could have dumped water over his head, and he would have been okay with that too. Todd's story had obviously touched him.

Chapter 28

Hospice

On Monday, I knew it was time to call in hospice. Todd still functioned without their help, but I wanted everything in place for when we really would need them. By now, Todd's stomach stuck way out in the front and even on the side. Back in November, when the tumor was the size of a football, it was barely noticeable. I couldn't begin to imagine how large it must be now. I know his stomach's size concerned him, but in typical Todd fashion, he did not say much about it.

On Tuesday, a hospice nurse and another worker came by our house. The nurse went into the living room with Todd to do a preliminary checkup. The other worker went over the large amount of paperwork I had to fill out. As we talked, she asked what they could do to meet Todd's needs. Confused, I asked her to explain what she meant. I was not sure whether they wanted to bring him a milkshake or a book or do something bigger. She assured me they would do anything at all, so I told her Todd wanted his room redecorated. I was not quite sure whether it was too big a request to mention, but she loved the idea. Todd and Jeffrey had shared the same room for years, and although I still loved the train border in their room, Todd had definitely outgrown it. He wanted something more exciting and age appropriate for a teenager!

Todd was especially excited to hear about the room makeover and eagerly anticipated taking part in the planning process. The joy on his face and knowing he had something to take his mind off his illness, if only for a while, made me happy.

On Wednesday, Todd's personal hospice nurse, Cindy, came to meet him and assess him. Given her job, I was not sure how Todd would take to her, but she had a fun personality and was sensitive without being morbid. She connected with him right away, and I knew she was the right person to take care of him. After spending some time with Todd, she talked with me privately about the prescriptions—including liquid morphine—she would have filled for me in case of emergency. She seemed to have everything under control. I had no idea how wonderful hospice could be for a family facing the death of a loved one. Whenever I heard the word *hospice*, I just thought about death. Calling in hospice seemed as if I was giving up hope that God would heal Todd. In reality, hospice was so much more than I ever dreamed it would be.

The next day two women—also hospice volunteers—arrived to give Todd a massage. They may not have realized what that massage meant to us because they do them so frequently, but I could see the relief it brought Todd. Once again God used the gentle touch of another person to help my precious son.

As the two women were leaving, Shannon, the decorator, arrived to discuss room plans with Todd and Jeffrey. I liked Shannon right away. I hadn't known exactly what to expect, but I assumed he would be businesslike and just there to do a job, maybe one he didn't want to do. Instead, I saw a man with a desire to bring some joy to a young man who did not have much time left on the earth.

Shannon asked Todd and Jeffrey specific questions about their desires for their room. Todd wanted the room to reflect his love for the Panthers football team, and Jeffrey wanted it to highlight his loyalty to the Clemson Tigers. Shannon listened carefully to them, and then he asked for my input. I could tell Shannon was a great decorator, so I left all the ideas up to him. With the boys' help, he came up with a paint combination on each side of the chair rail that represented both teams. I was happy Todd got to help choose the color he wanted in his room.

Shannon didn't waste any time getting started on the project. The next day, he painted the room and ordered window treatments, blinds, bedding, and wall decorations. We could not wait to see the room transformation.

Chapter 29

Final Gatherings

Todd's freshman class scheduled their year-end party at an outdoor pavilion for Monday, May 6. Todd had attended only about two months of first semester and just a couple days of second semester, but his classmates wanted to include him. Todd could walk from room to room in our house, but whenever we went out, he used a wheelchair. When we arrived at the party, Todd's friends ran over as I pushed him toward the pavilion. They were so excited to see him. He said, "Hello," but little else. I asked several different friends to pose for pictures with him, but still, he barely said a word. I watched Todd as he observed his friends playing basketball and soccer. My heart ached for him. How hard it must be for him to watch his friends, healthy and strong, while he sat in a wheelchair fighting for his very life.

At times, the conversation was awkward; understandably, some of his friends did not know what to say to him in his condition. Since Todd wasn't talking much, we didn't stay long. On the way home, I asked, "Todd, was it hard for you to see your friends?"

He responded softly, "Yes, it was." I waited. He didn't add anything else, but he didn't need to; I could see the sadness in his eyes.

On Wednesday, Todd's church youth group asked to come to our house to sing and pray with Todd. I thought their presence would lift his spirit and encourage him, so I agreed. Todd's friends eagerly greeted him when they arrived. His face lit up as everyone sat around him on the couch, on the floor, and in surrounding chairs. Conner, a friend of Todd's since they were infants, brought his guitar, and before long, the sound of guitar music and teens singing praises to the Lord filled our house. As usual, Todd sat on the couch with his legs drawn up by his stomach. I think the pressure relieved some of his pain. I loved seeing him surrounded by his friends, but the sight of his feet swollen twice their size bothered me.

Their evening together went quickly. Too soon, the teens prepared to sing their last song. When they asked Todd what he wanted everyone to sing, he requested "In Christ Alone," by Keith Getty and Stuart Townend. I studied Todd's face as he sang every single verse with them. The last stanza brought tears to my eyes because I knew, for Todd, in that moment, the words were true.

> No guilt in life, no fear in death—
> This is the power of Christ in me;
> From life's first cry to final breath,
> Jesus commands my destiny.
> No pow'r of hell, no scheme of man,
> Can ever pluck me from His hand;
> Till He returns or calls me home—
> Here in the pow'r of Christ I'll stand.

Todd chose a wonderful song to end the evening. The text is rich in meaning, and the teens sang with great enthusiasm. I loved these kids for the time they had invested in Todd's life. Some had visited him in the hospital, several had gathered around his hospital bed singing Christmas carols, many had sent him notes and cards, and some had even fasted to pray for his healing. Once again, God used human instruments to show our family His grace.

Chapter 30

Letting Go

Each morning when Todd woke up and walked into the living room, I silently prayed, *"Thank you, Lord . . . it's not today."* I believed that if he could still walk around, it surely would not be the day he died.

Todd had asked me a few days earlier whether he and I could go away for a night alone. I was all for the time alone together and decided I would use it as an opportunity to talk to him about how he felt about everything. We picked Thursday, May 9, and selected a hotel about two miles away. Not far, but we would be alone. Just before we were supposed to leave, I called my friend Debbie to wish her a happy birthday. After we talked for a while, I told her I had to get off the phone because Todd and I were going away. I looked at Todd as I spoke, and he shook his head no. Puzzled, I hung up. "Ok, let's go."

Todd responded in a tired voice, "Mom, I can't go."

"What do you mean?"

"I just can't go, I'm too tired."

Desperate for our special time together, I said, "Todd, all you have to do is walk out to the van. When we get to the hotel, I will take you up to the room in a wheelchair."

"I'm too tired. I can't go," he insisted.

Reluctantly, I gave in and agreed to stay home. As I had learned from our conversation weeks earlier, he was the one who truly knew how he felt inside. He wanted to stay home. I needed to respect his wishes.

A short time later, David took Brandon, Lauren, and Jeffrey to a friend's graduation party, leaving Todd and me alone in the house. He and I were sitting on the couch together, and without any thought, I said, "Todd, I need to talk to you."

I hadn't planned what to say, but the words flowed. "I know you don't like to talk about certain things, but I need to share some thoughts with you." I knew I had his attention so I proceeded. "I know you have trusted Jesus as your Savior, so I want to talk to you about heaven." In my heart, I chided myself for not asking him one more time to tell me about accepting Jesus as his Savior. I just wanted to make sure, one more time, that he was a Christian. I thought maybe I would come back to that subject later in our conversation. I continued, "Sometimes I wonder what the passing over part from earth to heaven will be like. I don't think it will be like being sucked up through a tube, not knowing where you are going or when you will arrive at your destination. I think it will be more like you will be sitting in the living room, blink your eyes, and in the next blink, you will wake up in heaven. It is my prayer that you will go from my arms to God's arms." I fought back tears as I continued. "Todd, if the Lord takes me to heaven before you, I promise to meet you at heaven's gate. If He takes you to heaven before me, you meet me at heaven's gate, okay?" Todd softly replied, "Okay."

I continued, "Todd, no one knows how long their time will be on this earth." I quoted Psalm 139:16: "Your eyes saw my unformed substance; in your book were written, every one of them, the days that were formed for me, when as yet there were none of them." My tears began to fall. "Todd, from the beginning of time, the Lord knew that you were going to be born on March 4, 1997, and He knows you are going to die on whatever day He chooses to take you home. Cancer will not cut your life short. Todd, if the Lord does choose to take you in the near future, you will not miss out on one single thing in this life. Nothing is more important here than what will take place in heaven. You won't miss us at all. The Bible says that one day with the Lord is as a thousand years. If you go first, you will be in heaven and then momentarily turn around and say to me, 'Oh, there you are.' For me, I will miss you for the rest of my life." I continued talking about the mansion God is preparing for each of us—how wonderful it will be to see one day—and about whom he would see in heaven—grandparents, my Auntie Jean, my cousin Mary, Uncle Bo, and our dear friend Stephen, who had lost his battle to cancer ten years ago. Since the doctor told me Jeffrey probably had a twin I lost soon after conception, I reminded him to look for someone who resembled his little brother. Todd smiled when I mentioned maybe seeing a brother in heaven.

Finally, I asked, "Todd, what do you hope will come from your illness?"

He replied with hope, "I just want to get better so that I can be a testimony for the Lord." This, not the trip to New York City, was Todd's true final wish. He wanted to be a testimony for the Lord.

"Todd, you already are a testimony for the Lord." I reminded him people watched him battle cancer, and his sweet response to his trial was the testimony God chose to use, not necessarily the healing. When I said these words, I noticed a change in his demeanor. It was as if at this point, he resigned himself to the fact that it was not the Lord's will to heal him in this lifetime. With a trembling voice, I told him, "Todd, when you don't feel like fighting anymore, you can go and be with the Lord." He quickly replied, "I'm worried about you."

"I'll be okay. If I ever find that I'm not okay, I'll get help. I promise."

I could not express much of this without tears, but I was thankful the Lord gave me the strength to speak. I added, "Todd, you are my hero, and I love you so much."

Then I asked, "Do you remember years ago when you told me when I got old you would spoon-feed me my jello?"

"Yes."

"I'm going to hold you to that."

In my heart I prayed, *"Please, let him live to do that for me, Lord."* I hoped in my heart Todd would reassure me that he would indeed be with me to spoon-feed me my jello one day, but he didn't say anything. I could see he was getting tired, and I felt I had said what needed to be said.

"Todd, we don't have to talk about this anymore, but can I hug you?"

He lovingly replied, "Yes." I gathered him in my arms, put my cheek next to his, and held him close for a few moments; his body felt so small and frail. How I loved my precious son.

He did not feel well and wanted to sleep in the living room that night, so I put a blanket down on the couch and covered him up. As always, I kissed him goodnight before I went to bed. As bad as things seemed, I clung to the small hope that God would heal Todd.

In the middle of the night, I heard Todd throwing up. I ran to the living room to help him. Watching him throw up volumes of green bile disheartened me. Little did I know, this marked the beginning of the end.

Chapter 31

Paradise

When we awoke the morning of May 10, 2013, we had no idea what was in store for us. David got up early to get ready for work just as Todd got sick once again. I gave him medicine for nausea, which helped some. David planned to go to the Cancer Clinic later to deliver a check from some of the proceeds raised on skate night. He wanted Todd to come with him and personally hand the doctors the check, but Todd told him he was too tired. David begged him to come. I put my hand on David's arm, "Honey, he said no." I know David was disappointed, but he didn't keep begging him.

Weeks earlier, we had taken individual pictures of Todd and several of the doctors and nurses. Now Todd did his best to sign the pictures with a special note to each one. David went to the clinic alone, where he passed out the pictures and presented the check. The staff appreciated the donation and promised to purchase something nice for the kids on the fifth floor. Todd specifically wanted a fish tank for the kids and hospital employees to enjoy.

That morning, while Todd rested on the couch, I decided I should send out a Facebook post to let people know about Todd's condition.

> Todd and I did not get to go away last night. His heart rate is very high, and blood pressure is very low. He is on oxygen now, which is making him feel comfortable. Our sweet hospice nurse is coming in regularly to make sure he stays comfortable. We were able to have a sweet chat last night alone, and I will always cherish our talk. Please pray for my sweet boy and for our family. I am learning a lot about real faith. It is not about snuggly feelings; it is

about fact. If God says it in His word, it is true. I haven't "arrived," but I am in the process of seeing that it is true. I love the fact that although Jesus was in the process of dying on the cross, He looked down at His mother and made sure that John would take care of her. I know Jesus knows a mother's heart. What a precious reunion He must have had with His mother. I am thankful that God has given me the privilege of being a mother to Brandon, Todd, Lauren, and Jeffrey. Please pray for strength in the days ahead and for peace for Todd's heart. He is my hero.

I looked over at my precious boy resting on the couch and wondered how much more time we had together.

Dr. John planned to come by for a quick visit that afternoon. When I told Todd, he said in a worried voice, "I don't want him to see my stomach."

I reassured him, "He isn't stopping by to examine you; he is just stopping by to see you as a friend." I know Todd could tell the tumor had grown significantly, and he knew Dr. John would recognize it as well.

David came home from his meeting at the hospital in time to greet Dr. John when he arrived. Thankfully, Todd had stopped throwing up, so he and Dr. John talked for a few minutes. Dr. John spent a few moments talking privately with David and me before going in to say goodbye to Todd. It was only 2:15, but Todd was falling asleep. I heard Dr. John say, "That's okay; get some rest, and I'll see you later."

When David and I sat down to eat lunch, Todd was sleeping. This was strange; Todd never slept during the day. David asked me whether I thought he should go back to work. Although I couldn't put my finger on my reasoning, I told him that I thought it was best if he stayed home for the rest of the day. When I went into the living room to check on Todd, he tried to talk to me, but all he did was mumble incoherently. This was a sudden change in his behavior.

I immediately called Cindy, the hospice nurse, to relay my concern about Todd. A short time later, she arrived to examine him. After she listened to his heart, she told me the rate was quite high. That news didn't surprise me; an elevated heart rate had been somewhat normal for Todd in the last few months. Cindy told me this usually indicates someone is actively dying, but he was too alert for that to be the case. She sat with us for a while before leaving to run an errand. She promised to return as soon as possible.

In the meantime, my sister, Corinne, sensed she needed to come over to see Todd. She told her husband, Andy, about the feeling; he told her he had felt the same way. When they arrived, David met them at the door with the news that Todd was deteriorating rapidly. We did not know what would happen, but David and I felt it was best not to have Lauren and Jeffrey remain at home. Corinne took them to visit friends, and then she returned to our house. Before Lauren and Jeffrey left, they both kissed Todd on the forehead and told him they loved him. In a weak voice, without opening his eyes, he whispered, "I love you too." None of us knew it would be the last time they would see him alive.

Cindy returned from her errand within two hours and listened to Todd's chest again. This time, she looked into my eyes and said, "I think Todd is actively dying."

Without letting her words sink in completely, I urged David to call our parents so that they could see Todd one more time. I asked Andy to contact Brent and his family in South Africa to let them know Todd was declining. I did not want them to find out any information from Facebook. Andy also called Pastor Danny and Kristen, who arrived a short time later.

Meanwhile, Trey and Shawn had the same overwhelming feeling Corinne and Andy had had; they needed to see Todd. When Trey and Shawn arrived, Todd had stopped mumbling incoherently. He appeared to be sleeping, but if someone asked him a question, he answered. When Shawn joked with Todd about eating steak together, he responded, "With A.1."

In the midst of all that was happening, his remark struck me as funny. If he were going to have steak, he had to make sure it would have his A.1. sauce on it! Shawn's own father was close to death, and she wanted to get back to his bedside, but she had a hard time leaving Todd. Her love and compassion for him was obvious. At one point she left, only to come back minutes later saying she just could not leave him.

Later in the evening, I sat at the foot of the couch holding Todd's icy cold feet in my hands. To warm them, I put my red fleecy slipper socks on his feet. After a while, Todd opened his eyes, and said clearly, "I want you to please put on the music." We had had beautiful Christian music playing earlier in the day, and he wanted it turned back on. Later, he opened his eyes again, looked directly at me and whispered, "I want you to put your cheeks right here." He pointed to his side. I moved at his direction, got on my knees, and took his hands in mine. I never saw him open his eyes again. Guests came and went. When they leaned over to hug me, I snuggled up to them, but I did not let go of my boy's hands.

Cindy warned me, saying, "Todd could go on in this condition for days." I silently prayed, *"Please, Lord . . . no . . . "* Cindy offered to spend the night with us to help watch over Todd. Whenever she sensed Todd was uncomfortable, she administered morphine. To me, Todd appeared calm and peaceful the whole time.

My mother prepared Lauren's room for Cindy to spend the night, while David, Brandon, Corinne, Andy, Danny, and Kristen talked at the kitchen table. As I held Todd's hands, I whispered in his ear, "Todd, you're my hero and I love you so much. Can you tell me that you love me?"

"I love you," Todd whispered softly.

"When you don't feel like fighting anymore, you can go and be with Jesus. I'll be okay." In reality, I could not imagine how I could possibly be okay without him, but he needed to hear those words. I sang to him just loud enough so only he could hear me; not knowing what my voice sounded like and hoping he didn't care that it wasn't beautiful. I asked, "Todd, can you see heaven?"

He did not respond.

"Do you see pretty flowers or angels?"

Still, no words.

"Can you hear music?"

Again, he did not answer, and I felt troubled.

Finally, I asked, "Todd, do you see Jesus?"

Slowly and deliberately, he whispered softly, "Not. Yet."

I rested my cheek on our clasped hands. Moments later, I felt his thumb rub over mine two or three times, gently, but purposefully. Todd had never done that to me before. Scared, I wondered what he was trying to tell me. I was afraid to look at him.

Suddenly, he made a gargling sound in his throat. I lifted my head up and called out to Cindy, who was seated nearby. "What's that noise? I don't like it."

Calmly she said, "Let me listen to his chest."

She positioned her stethoscope over his heart and immediately called out, "Oh my goodness, tell everyone to come." She ran out of the room, leaving Todd and me alone. The moment she left the room, I looked at Todd's face. His shoulders lifted up, his head rolled back, and something began pouring out of his nose and mouth. I thought he was throwing up again. Everyone in the house rushed into the room. Frantic, I asked, "What's happening?"

"Put your head down," Cindy ordered. I held Todd's hands and rested my cheek on them, repeating, "What's happening? What's happening?"

Soon I felt David's hands on my shoulders and Brandon's hands on me as well. Everyone in the room kept urging David, Brandon, and me to keep our heads lowered. In a few moments, Cindy softly spoke the words I had dreaded since our ordeal began.

"He's gone."

I went into shock. I heard myself crying out to God, but I was powerless to stop. With my eyes still closed, I cried out with a guttural voice, "Are you sure? Jesus, do you have my baby? You didn't tell me You were taking my baby. I don't know where he is. I'm so sorry, Todd." In agony, I repeated the words over and over. I was later told that while I cried out to the Lord, Cindy, Corinne, and Kristen used five bath towels to soak up the blood that poured out of Todd's mouth, even after he died.

As God ordained, Danny rushed into the room with everyone else when Cindy yelled for them to come. After several minutes, in the midst of my cries, his voice rose above every other sound in the room.

Purposefully, he called out my name, "Brenda! Everything we need from God is in His Word. His Word is enough. You don't need a sign."

In those frantic moments, I never cried out to God that I needed a sign, but that was exactly what I was looking for. I wanted Todd to tell me he saw glimpses of heaven, and I wanted him to describe what he was seeing. I have heard of other people, who on their deathbed, describe heaven as it is coming into their view. I had wanted to hear Todd's description so that I could know he was going to heaven. As Danny pointed out, I did not need a sign to know; I needed to take God at His Word. Romans 10:13 says, "For everyone who calls on the name of the Lord will be saved." Todd had asked Jesus to forgive him of his sins and be his Savior as a young child. Whether or not he talked about heaven on his deathbed was not proof of his salvation. With Danny's reminder, my heart moved from turmoil to peace within seconds.

David, Brandon, and I kept our heads down until Cindy said, "Ok, you can lift your head." I immediately looked at Todd's chest. His heart had worked so hard the past few days that I could literally see it beating in his chest. It was still now. I looked at his precious face. His eyes were shut and his mouth was motionless. I could not believe my baby was gone.

David kept his arm around me for a while and then got up and called our friend Randy, who we had prearranged to be our funeral director when the time came. Randy and his wife, Ashley, had been part of our Shepherding Group (a group of families that meet together in private homes bi-monthly to share burdens and pray) at church, and they were our dear friends. Randy was our only choice to prepare Todd's body for the funeral.

Our long-time friends, Peter and Karen, arrived at our house just moments after Todd died. Peter and I had been in boarding school together, and he was like a brother to me. Their presence comforted me at just the right time. Danny and Peter prayed. There was no more shock or chaos, just peace.

When Randy and Ashley arrived, Randy lovingly took command of the situation. "Take all the time you want with Todd, but when you are ready for me to take him, I want you to go into your room. I don't think it's a good idea for you to watch me take him out of the house."

I had held Todd's hands for hours, now they were cold and formed around mine. The hardest thing I had to do was let go of his hands, but I knew it was time. Kissing them, I placed them gently on his chest. I stood up, kissed Todd on the forehead, and went to my room as Randy requested. Within a few minutes, Randy knocked on my bedroom door. "Brenda, you can come out now."

I immediately went to the front door and stepped out onto the porch. I wanted to honor Todd by watching the car drive him away from our house. It was about eleven, and I was thankful for the darkness. I didn't know whether our neighbors were aware of what was going on, and I knew seeing a body bag being removed from our house would unsettle them. David joined me on the porch, and we talked with Randy for a few minutes. He said he would come over in the morning to discuss the funeral arrangements. As he started walking down the street toward his car, I told him I was going to watch him drive away with Todd.

Randy gently informed me that his business partner had taken Todd's body away a few minutes earlier. I was disappointed, but not upset; no one had known I wanted to watch him leave.

Shortly after Todd passed away, Corinne picked Lauren up from her friend's house. She broke the news to Lauren before she came home. When Corinne pulled the car into our driveway, Lauren came out of the car sobbing, and I quickly gathered her in my arms.

"I'm so sorry, Lauren. When you left earlier today, we didn't know Todd was going to die. I'm so glad you kissed him goodbye and told him you loved him."

Lauren sobbed, "Yeah, but I didn't tell him enough."

I think she was scared to be in the house and wanted to stay with her cousins, but I needed our family to be together.

Andy brought Jeffrey home in another car. When David and I told him Todd had died, he looked troubled, but he did not cry. He didn't know how to process the news. I was having a hard time processing Todd's death myself.

One by one, our family and friends left and we were alone. David and I hugged and comforted Brandon, Lauren, and Jeffrey, and tucked them into bed. I felt numb and exhausted. It was late, and I did not know anything else to do but try to sleep myself. As I lay in bed, I read the May 10 entry of *Streams in the Desert*, a book of daily Scripture readings and lessons. The Scripture was Psalm 27:13–14: "I believe that I shall look upon the goodness of the Lord. . . . Wait for the Lord; be strong, and let your heart take courage." The entry seemed fitting for the day's events. In the accompanying lesson, the author recounted Hudson Taylor's last days. "Hudson Taylor was so weak and feeble in the last few months of his life that he told a friend, 'I am so weak I cannot write. I cannot read my Bible. I cannot even pray. All I can do is lie still in the arms of God as a little child, trusting Him.' This wonderful man of God came to the point of physical suffering and weakness where all he could do was lie still and trust" [188].

I was not dying like Hudson Taylor, but I was emotionally, physically, and spiritually drained. I had just enough strength to pray, *"Lord, . . . help."* I wrapped myself in the blanket that had covered Todd all throughout that long, painful day. With tears streaming down my cheeks, I fell asleep.

Chapter 32

Plans and Provisions

I woke up and looked at the clock. It was 5:20. The reality of Todd's death immediately began to sink in, and my tears began to flow. Randy was coming to talk to us about funeral arrangements, so I didn't let myself cry for long. I had to get up and face the day. I walked into the living room to find Gracie up on the couch resting her head on the pillow that had been Todd's just the night before. She looked so pitiful. I have heard it said that animals sense our emotions. As I studied her face, I recalled that I hadn't heard her bark a single time yesterday. She always barked when people came to the door, but not yesterday. I sat beside her and lovingly scratched her behind her ear. "Gracie, did you know Todd met Jesus last night? Did Jesus tell you that you needed to be a good dog and not bark?" Gracie was normally extremely playful—especially in the morning, but not today. She seemed unusually quiet. I snuggled up next to her as tears streamed down my cheeks and onto her fur.

Around 10 a.m. the doorbell rang. I looked out to find a beautiful white floral arrangement on the door and Randy standing on the porch with a freshly baked coconut cake. Surprised, but touched by his kindness, I thanked him and invited him inside. He told me that for some reason he woke up at 5:20 and couldn't sleep, so he decided to make us a cake. I thought God was so kind to lay it on Randy's heart to prepare something comforting for us at the very moment my heart was breaking. Random acts of kindness like this happened over and over again during our journey.

Before we discussed the funeral arrangements, there was something I needed to know.

"Where is Todd, Randy?" Randy worked at two different funeral homes and I needed to know exactly where he was. Randy responded, very kindly and with a compassionate smile, "He's with me."

I was so glad to hear his response. I knew Todd was in heaven, but the way Randy answered me with those words comforted me greatly. It was as if he was protecting Todd in a way that I couldn't protect him.

"Thank you, Randy. That makes me so happy. When are you going to prepare his body?"

"I did it last night."

I was surprised at his answer. Randy did not leave our house until nearly eleven, so he had stayed up until the wee hours with Todd.

" Do you always work that quickly?"

"Not always. I just wanted to do it right away so he would look good."

Again, his words were incredibly comforting to me. I had taken care of Todd his whole life. Now I couldn't do for Todd what needed to be done—it was out of my hands as a mother—yet his care was entrusted to a dear friend and I was at peace.

Randy asked me for some clothes for Todd's burial. The choice was simple. I wanted Todd dressed in jeans and one of his favorite polo shirts, a pink one with wide navy blue stripes. I also wanted Todd to wear his glasses and a yellow bracelet with the word "Strength" imprinted on it. Katie "MacLurtey" had given Todd this bracelet while he was in the hospital, and he wore it all the time. Before Randy closed the casket for the final time, he would collect the bracelet and glasses for me.

David and I planned to have the viewing and service at our church; we wanted to be in a place that brought us comfort. I asked Randy and his wife, Ashley, to sit with our Shepherding Group right behind us during the service. We settled a few more details before Randy left.

"Take good care of my boy," I called out to him.

"I will," he promised me with a smile. I knew he meant it.

Later that morning, Danny and Kristen came over to discuss the funeral service with David and me. We selected songs that were particularly meaningful to us, as well as a passage of Scripture that has always been special to me—Psalm 139. Danny asked whether I wanted him to talk about anything in particular during the sermon. He had ideas about what he wanted to say, but he wanted our input.

"Please talk about John 11. I don't understand that passage at all."

The Lord healed Lazarus, so I could not understand why He didn't heal Todd. I definitely wanted Danny to talk about why God said no to so many people who prayed for the same answer—that God would heal Todd.

I also wanted him to address Todd's school and church friends. Many of them prayed for Todd as they had for Jona, the other student who had died of cancer two years earlier. Why should they keep praying for healing when God did not seem to answer them? I would not know how to answer that question, so it was important to me that Danny help them as they struggled with the death of another classmate.

Before Danny and Kristen left, David and I shared some funny Todd stories that we might want my brother Brent to include in the eulogy we had asked him to give. Danny and Kristen knew Todd his entire life, and our families had been together on numerous occasions, so we reminisced and even laughed together as we planned Todd's funeral.

Although in the week between Todd's death and funeral there were many funeral details to keep us occupied, Todd was a constant part of my thoughts. Mother's Day came less than 48 hours after Todd passed away. I felt as if I were living in a fog. A mother should celebrate with all her children, but one of mine was missing. I didn't just cry all day, but I definitely had a hole in my heart. I comforted myself by thinking, *"Todd is with Randy."* Of course, I knew he was actually with the Lord. Brandon, Lauren, and Jeffrey wanted to take a picture with me, but I could not bear having one without Todd, so I grabbed a photo of him and held it in my hands. With tears in my eyes, and as much of a smile as I could muster, we took a picture.

The next day, Brent and his family were scheduled to arrive from South Africa for the funeral. While we waited for them at the airport, I called friends to ask whether they would serve as Todd's pallbearers. Without exception, each man responded to my question with the words, "It would be an honor."

As I made phone calls, my eyes were glued to the passengers disembarking from various airplanes. Finally, Brent and his family descended the escalator stairs. I was thrilled to see all of them, but as soon as I reached my big brother's arms, I dissolved into tears. He loved Todd and Todd loved him. I was sorry Brent and his family didn't get one final goodbye but was so thankful for the Disney trip we had taken together in September and for the time Brent spent with Todd in Charleston in November. The Lord knew the future that we could not see and blessed us with a time to take lots of extended family pictures and make special memories.

In the midst of all the plans we had to make, I was thankful we did not have to worry about buying the cemetery plot and casket. Wisely, David prearranged these purchases, and we had already decided together where to bury Todd if the Lord chose not to heal him. One option was a cemetery several miles from our home. Burying Todd there would have been significantly cheaper, but I wanted Todd near me, so we settled on a closer location. Having these details already in place gave us one less detail to think about that week and it was a blessing.

Wednesday morning I ordered flowers for Todd's casket, one of the few things I did for the funeral. Purchasing flowers for my son's funeral seemed so wrong, but I wanted to be the one to select them. I knew I wanted something pretty, yet masculine. Todd would not appreciate girly flowers on his casket. While I waited for the florist to finish with another customer, I leafed through several books before I found an arrangement I thought would have pleased Todd. When my turn came, and the florist asked what she could do to help me, the tears began to flow. "I'm here to purchase flowers for my son's casket." Thankfully, the florist helped plan Todd's arrangement with expertise and compassion. In addition to the casket spray, I ordered a single white rose to lay on Todd's chest. The white rose would be a symbol of Jesus's victory over death.

Randy suggested David and I see Todd's body on Wednesday before the formal viewing Thursday evening. David and I went to the funeral home alone at first. I was anxious to see my boy; I missed him so much. In the funeral home lobby, Randy had a desk with one of Todd's recent school pictures and a candle burning beside the picture. David and Randy stood in the lobby talking, but I needed to see Todd. Entering the room Randy pointed out, I found my precious boy in a casket. Seeing him that way was surreal.

Touching or even seeing a dead body may trouble some people, but this was my Todd. I leaned down, kissed him, and wrapped my arms around him. I was glad to look at him again. We had been together almost continually since September, and I had not seen him in several days. Randy did a great job preparing Todd's body; he looked wonderful to me. After chemo, Todd had worn a hat for months. Even though his hair had started growing back before he died, it was still sparse, so Randy filled it in with color. His eyebrows and long eyelashes had grown back in so Todd looked more like he did before cancer. I studied his features. I put my hands on his and memorized the feel of them. They were cold, which saddened me; his hands had always been warm. Finally, David joined me by the casket and wrapped a comforting arm around me. We both lovingly gazed down at our precious son, lost in our private thoughts.

David left me at the funeral home for a short time to pick up Brandon, Lauren, and Jeffrey. We had no idea how they would react, so we agreed they should see Todd before the Thursday night visitation. I savored my time alone with Todd, studying his features, kissing his forehead, and always touching his hand. When David returned with Brandon, Lauren, and Jeffrey, they cautiously approached the casket. None of them spoke, but all of them reached out to touch him. They didn't know what to say or think. His death had not fully sunk in with any of us. The body in the casket looked like Todd, but we all thought, *"How can this be true? How can this lifeless body be our Todd?"*

Still, my heart was mostly peaceful. All my children were with me again. Our family was together. When we had to leave, I was grateful I would see Todd again the next day.

Brenda Lurtey

Chapter 33

Viewing

Late Thursday afternoon we arrived at the church for the viewing. Two of my dearest friends from boarding school, Lois and Diane, greeted us at the front door. They wrapped me in their arms with comforting hugs. Within a few minutes, the hearse arrived with our precious son's body. I stood in the hallway watching as the closed casket was wheeled into the sanctuary. I stayed back until Randy had the casket open and the coverings situated. The moment the casket was ready, I eagerly went to Todd. I kissed his forehead and held his hand. I studied his features once again. Tears fell as I placed my forehead next to his. How I would miss Todd. I wished this were a terrible dream I could wake from, but it was not. This was reality. David stood next to me with his arm around my shoulder. Brandon, Lauren, and Jeffrey all approached the casket and reached down to touch Todd once again. We spent some time together by the casket before retreating to another room.

I was sitting in a private area when the MacDonald family arrived. Shawn's father was in the last stages of his life, and she usually stayed by his bedside. It meant a lot to us that they came to pay their respects to Todd and comfort our family when they were preparing to mourn their own loss. I could tell Shawn's heart was breaking when she saw Todd's body. The MacDonalds are dear friends, and we have so many family memories as the "MacLurteys." A very important person was forever gone from our close-knit group, and the resulting pain ran deep. Shawn and I held on to one another and cried. Neither one of us could speak.

Before visitation began, our extended family ate a quick meal lovingly prepared by Diane and Lois with money provided by several of my high school classmates. It was a relief not to worry about preparing food. After supper, the family gathered around the casket before the doors opened to the public. Earlier that day, each immediate family member had written a personal message to Todd; now we placed our notes inside the casket.

Dear Todd: I love you so much, and I miss you Todd. I know you love me too, Todd. It's not the same without you, Todd. I wish you were still with us. I miss you. Love, Jeffrey

Dear Todd: I love you and miss you so much. You will always have a special place in my heart. Love your little sis, Lauren Lurtey

Dear Todd: Thanks for being a great brother to me. I will cherish the memories we made together forever. I love you! I am sorry that you suffered through this trial, but I am glad you are not suffering anymore! See you soon! Love, Brandon

Todd, you were such a trooper during your illness. I don't know if I could have endured everything you went through. Thanks for being a wonderful son to me. I love you! Dad

To My Sweet Todd: You have run your race with patience. You have finished your course with joy. You have kept the faith. You are my hero! No more pain! Because you placed your trust in Jesus to be your Savior, and because He won the victory over death—that victory is yours! I'm honored to be your mom! Until we meet at heaven's gate—just like we talked about. We will miss you and love you always. Your Proud Mom

Randy put my note in Todd's hands along with the single white rose. Todd was gone, but death had not defeated him. Because Todd knew

Jesus as his Savior, he was alive in heaven; death was swallowed up in victory.

As the first visitors came into the sanctuary, I silently prayed, *"Lord, help!"* Visitation was scheduled for three-and-a-half hours. Our family would stand together beside Todd one last time and thank our guests for all the prayers and love they showered on us over the past seven months. I was not sure how I would feel. Would I cry all night? Would I hold myself together? I did not know. In truth, it helped to have people come through to show they cared. After people greeted us, many sat down to watch a slideshow of family pictures David and our friend Del had made. To accompany the pictures, David selected songs that had comforted us throughout Todd's illness.

I've always thought viewings can be uncomfortable. Greeting the family can be awkward; guests often feel pressured to come up with great words of wisdom or comfort. Todd's friends were the hardest for us to see; teenagers do not typically have to pay their last respects to their friends. One of Todd's dearest friends came through the line with his father. His chin quivered and he looked directly at me with big tears in his eyes, unable to say a word. My heart ached for him and the loss I knew he felt. I hugged him, thanked him for coming, and assured him Todd loved him very much. I realized during Todd's viewing that what people say is not what matters the most. Just their presence showed they cared about our family, and that was important to our family. God gave us incredible strength during the visitation. Although we cried at times, the evening was primarily a celebration of Todd's life with the people who loved and prayed for him.

Chapter 34

Until We Meet at Heaven's Gate

A funeral limo arrived at 11:30 to take us to the church. I wondered how we would get through the day, but I knew God was with us. The casket was already in place at the front of the church when we arrived. I immediately made my way to the casket to spend one last private moment with Todd. I stared at Todd's precious face, kissed him, and rested my forehead against his. I laid my hands on his cold hands. I did not want to stop touching him.

When the slide show started, David and I went back into a secluded room with the rest of our family to wait for the funeral to begin. At 1:45, Randy escorted David and me to the front of the church for the closing of the casket. I have never liked that funeral directors close the casket without any family members present; I have always thought a relative should be the last person on earth to view the loved one. The slideshow and music from the night of the viewing were playing in the sanctuary as people filed into the church. Randy tucked in the bedding and removed Todd's glasses and yellow "Strength" bracelet. David stood with his arm around me as I kissed Todd one last time, leaving a lipstick mark on his forehead. We took a step back and Randy closed the casket lid. Knowing I would never see my child's face again in this lifetime was incredibly painful.

We returned to the room where Brandon, Lauren, Jeffrey, and the rest of our family waited. At two, we lined up behind Pastor Danny. He asked everyone in the sanctuary to rise, and we walked down the aisle. I could not focus on individual faces, but I was overwhelmed with gratitude as I noticed that the church was packed with people supporting our family and paying their last respects to Todd. Pastor Danny choked up a bit as he welcomed everyone to the service. My heart went out to him. He had held Todd in his arms as an infant and dedicated him to the Lord, stood beside him as an eight-year-old Todd gave his testimony, and baptized him moments later. Pastor Danny had supported Todd—and our whole family—through his illness, and now it was time to bury him. This was the first time Danny had had to bury a child from his congregation, and I could tell it affected him. Despite his personal grief, he spoke with grace and compassion.

> On behalf of the Lurteys, thank you. On behalf of Todd, thank you. Your presence here today is such a gift of God's grace. I know it's an outpouring of your love for them, and so many of you have poured it out over months now. It's just impossible to recount all the ways you have shown the love and kindness of the Lord Jesus, so thank you, and thank you for coming today. We have so many things to celebrate. And we feel that mixture of joy and sorrow. We are here to give praise and honor to the Lord Jesus Christ and to honor Todd and to be a blessing and support to his family.

Todd's funeral began with a beautiful song about heaven entitled "Somewhere Beyond the Moon" by Michael O'Brien, Leonard Ahlstrom, and Eddie Carswell. I closed my eyes and pictured Todd running down the streets of gold, full of life and without pain.

> Long ago and far away
> Before the laws of time and space
> A loving God prepared a place
> Somewhere beyond the moon
>
> High above this world's façade
> A perfect world where angels trod
> The hope of man, the home of God

Somewhere beyond the moon

Somewhere beyond all doubt and fear
Beyond the reach of sorrow's tears
Where broken hearts run strong and free
Where every child of God will be

Somewhere tonight someone will pray
Lord, you are the truth, the way
And on the streets of gold they celebrate
Somewhere beyond the moon

For every heart that will believe God's promises are true
There is a place called heaven He has prepared for you
As sure as there's a morning sun and stars up in the sky
One day we will see Jesus

Listen now, can you hear
The voice of God, calling clear
Saying Don't lose heart, the time is near
And we'll be goin' soon
Somewhere beyond the moon

At the conclusion of the song Todd's youth pastor, Abe, read Psalm 139, the chapter that I claimed for our family. As he read the chapter, I quoted the Scripture along with him as I had committed much of that chapter to memory. Following the Scripture reading, Brent walked up to the platform to give the eulogy. Todd loved Brent so much, and I was honored to see my brother stand in front of our church and give a tribute to Todd:

> I want to explain to you our memories of Todd, who he is, and why we cherished our time with him. Todd is one of those people that brought life to the party, that brought a smile to the situation, and that brought energy to the

group. He was one of those people that loved life and wanted to experience all of it. Burned in my mind and something that I will never forget is that dazzling smile of his that announced his presence.

When that big toothy grin was thrust in my face, the next words would often be this: "Hey Uncle Bunny [Bunny is a playful nickname I gave to my brother when we were young], can we go and play baseball or can we go and jump on the trampoline or play Killer Bunnies?" I cannot think of one time that Todd called me Uncle Brent. I was always Uncle Bunny to him.

This past summer we had the privilege of taking Todd and Brandon with us to a camp where I was speaking. Todd was so excited to go to this camp. We brought him and Brandon down to the cabin where they were going to be staying. Todd dropped off his stuff and took off. I was walking back to the car and received a phone call from my wife telling me that my oldest son, Kyle, was just diagnosed with Influenza B and we would all need to be quarantined for the next twenty-four hours. We were sequestered in this little chalet across the pond from the camp with three beds and seven people, one of whom was very sick, to sleep in those three beds. The kids were going stir crazy and would stand on the shore across from where the campers were, and they would holler, "We know you're having fun over there, but we have electronic devices over here!" For the next twenty-four hours Todd and Skyler [Brent's son] played games and even invented the game of pinecone baseball. When the twenty-four hours were over, Todd was off running and shouting, "We're free, we're free!" Then came the words, "Hey Uncle Bunny, will you climb the rock wall with me? Can we go canoeing?"

I smiled and recalled my own memories as Brent told some other funny family stories about Todd's enjoyment of life and some of his random thoughts. It was comforting to reminisce about happy times even in the midst of the sorrow we were facing.

Brent continued, "I hope you can see that Todd enjoyed life. He had a unique perspective on life, but he also had a serious side to him."

Brent then recounted the five days my sister-in-law, Susan, spent watching seven of the ten cousins while David and I were away celebrating our twentieth anniversary. Todd had opted to take a high school summer school course, so Susan had some alone time with him as she made him breakfast and drove him to school that week. She cherished the time she had with him.

Brent continued with his eulogy, leaving the funny side of Todd's life and entering the more serious side of Todd. He spoke about the beautiful displays that my friend, Jenny, had set up in our church lobby. Among the memorabilia were several of his papers that he had written. One of the papers detailed what he hoped he would be doing in ten years. Todd loved Christian movies and hoped to produce his own movies with a biblical perspective in the future. He also wrote papers about the possibility of being a missionary one day. "Todd had a passion to convey a message. While he loved life and enjoyed every second of it, he also understood some of the seriousness of life." Brent wanted to conclude his eulogy with one last memory to illustrate his point. He recounted our extended family trip to Disney World and in particular the evening when he took Todd and Skyler to the extra after hours in the park. Todd and Skyler asked Brent whether they could go off on their own. Since Todd was fifteen at the time and was showing some signs of maturity, Brent wanted to encourage him. After giving Todd very specific instructions about where they could go and the necessity of calling Brent to report back to him after each ride, they were entrusted with this special privilege. Todd did exactly what he was told to do. "Todd demonstrated to me some growing maturity. I can't help but wonder whether God was preparing him for a coming test with cancer that would demand real maturity, real maturity to face uncertainty and eternity with faith and confidence. I know, myself, that I don't know how I would have gone through this—the pendulum swings of going back and forth."

Brent recounted the first time Todd complained that his side hurt. We gave him Tylenol, and he was off and running again. He then told about returning to Africa at the end of their furlough. They had been back in Africa for two weeks when they learned that Todd had cancer. They had hope because we had a plan for treatment. Later, they felt great fear when we learned the tumor had doubled in size; yet once again there was hope with the plan for tumor resection in Charleston. "Through the whole thing, Todd was faithful and that smile was there," Brent recounted.

Hope faded yet again when we learned that the tumor had returned, and there was nothing that could be done for Todd. Todd left the hospital in early February to live out his remaining days at home. " I remember on Easter Brenda called, and there was Todd on Skype looking at me and smiling. Later I said to my wife, 'He looks better than he's ever looked. What's going on?" The pendulum continued its swing back and forth as weeks later Brent and his family received the news that Todd was not doing well and that he may not be with us for much longer. Brent continued:

> I don't know how Todd went through it except by the grace of God. Todd demonstrated something to me as a sixteen year old and that is, how to live life well, how to face death well, and how to live for Jesus. Psalm 23 says, "Even though I walk through the valley of the shadow of death, I will fear no evil, for you are with me; your rod and your staff, they comfort me. You prepare a table before me in the presence of my enemies; you anoint my head with oil; my cup overflows. Surely goodness and mercy shall follow me all the days of my life, and I shall dwell in the house of the Lord forever."

Brent tearfully concluded his eulogy.

I want to say thank you, Todd, for a life well-lived. I want to say thank you to my Heavenly Father for the privilege of sixteen years with Todd. I want to say thank you to Brenda and Dave, Brandon, Lauren, and Jeffrey for walking with Todd through this valley of death. I want to say thank you to all of you for sharing this burden with them. I pray that when my time comes for my home-going that I will face death and eternity with the same confidence that the author David wrote about in Psalm 23 and Todd demonstrated.

The service was everything David and I wanted it to be. The music was beautiful and meaningful. Brent's eulogy was heartfelt and, at times, even funny. Pastor Danny spoke movingly from John 11. His words were powerful, but I couldn't fully comprehend the message with all the emotions in my heart. All too soon, Danny concluded his sermon, prayed, and then nodded to the men in the sound booth to start the recessional music. Todd's funeral was over; it was time to leave.

This was the hardest part of the day so far. We would never again sit together as a family. Every memory we had together in our church was ending. I did not want anyone to take Todd out of the church where he had attended the nursery, kid's clubs, and youth group. I never wanted this to end for him. I did not want anyone to take Todd to the cemetery and put his body in the ground. I watched as my son's casket was wheeled out of the church. The pallbearers, all specifically chosen because of their investment in Todd's life, followed the casket out of church. Each man sadly hung his head. Our Shepherding Group had supported us, faithfully praying for Todd and for us during his illness, and now they were with us for the hardest part of all—walking through the valley of the shadow of death. Our family followed them out of the sanctuary. As we walked out, Amy, Todd's hospital social worker, ran up to us and pulled us into a hug, telling us the service was beautiful. We were so honored she had come to Todd's funeral. After a few tender words with Amy, we took our position in the funeral procession that would take Todd's body to its final resting place.

Chapter 35

Burial

The long ride to the cemetery seemed endless, but at the same time, I was in no hurry to get through this last part. I kept my eyes focused on the hearse carrying the body of our precious son. I did not want any other vehicle to get between the hearse and our car. Once we arrived at the cemetery, a sign reading "Lurtey" directed the processional to Todd's burial plot. Seeing our name on the sign seemed strange. I thought, *"Our name doesn't belong there."* We arrived at the plot and watched while the pallbearers removed Todd's casket from the hearse and positioned it on top of the vault. Our family took our seats under the funeral tent.

Pastor Danny stepped forward to begin the graveside service. "You know, one of the great comforts is the testimony of the individual who speaks clearly and lives with clarity so that we don't have to wonder, 'What did Todd believe?' His testimony was crystal clear. It was a great privilege to baptize him almost eight years ago. I have a handwritten copy of his testimony that he sent me before his baptism. It reads, 'Dear Pastor Brooks: This is how I got saved. I was thinking about how other people are getting saved and I thought that I should be saved, so I got saved. And I love God with my heart. It's because Jesus died on the cross for our sins.'" Pastor Brooks smiled and continued. "That's the simplest expression. There is more for us to find comfort in than just that Todd said I believe these things. Todd would have never submitted his heart in that way unless Christ had first spoken words of eternal life, called us to believe, and given us reason to believe. We take comfort in Todd's testimony, but we find even greater comfort in the words of God Himself."

Pastor Danny then read 2 Corinthians 4: 5–7 and 17, verses that spoke directly to my heart. "For what we proclaim is not ourselves, but Jesus

Christ as Lord, with ourselves as your servants for Jesus' sake. For God, who said, 'Let light shine out of darkness,' has shone in our hearts to give the light of the knowledge of the glory of God in the face of Jesus Christ. But we have this treasure in jars of clay, to show that the surpassing power belongs to God and not to us. . . . For this slight momentary affliction is preparing for us an eternal weight of glory beyond all comparison." In closing, he reminded us we would be together with Todd one day. I longed for that reunion with all my heart.

The graveside service was brief—too brief for me. I did not want to leave. Pastor Danny invited everyone to stay with our family for the actual burial; in my heart I felt our presence was the last thing we could do to honor Todd. Each family member placed a rose on top of the casket before moving off to the side. Everyone stood silently and watched as Todd's casket was slowly lowered into the vault, and the vault was lowered into the ground. How I wanted to hug Todd one more time. The casket seemed unsteady as it disappeared into the ground, and I worried the workers would accidentally drop it. Too soon, they began shoveling dirt on top of the vault. Watching was agonizing for me. Irrational thoughts flooded my mind. *"What if dirt gets in his nose and he can't breathe? What if he just seemed to be dead, but really wasn't?"* I desperately wanted someone to check on Todd one more time, just to see if we had made a huge mistake. My thoughts screeched to a halt as a machine, sounding like a jackhammer, began packing the dirt down over the casket.

I didn't notice much of anything going on around me, but when Randy pulled away in his car, I really hurt inside. *"Todd is not with Randy anymore, and he is not with me anymore. He's all alone."* As these thoughts threatened to overwhelm me, the Lord quickly reminded me that Todd's shell was the only thing in the ground. His spirit was with Him. I had to remember that.

After the burial, the limo took us back to the church where dear friends and family waited to share the funeral meal with us. By now, it was nearly four and we were starving. As we ate the tasty and nourishing food, we reminisced about Todd and our hearts were comforted. Finally, we could put it off no longer; we had to go home. Our new life without Todd was about to begin, and I could not fathom it.

Brenda Lurtey

Chapter 36

Adjustments and Anger

The next day I went back to the cemetery. At the head of the plot, Randy had placed a marker with Todd's name. A small gesture, but it meant so much to me. Without that placard, no one would know who rested beneath the soil—at least not until the permanent marker was in place. I sat down and let the tears flow. I had studied Todd so much in the casket that I could picture exactly how he was resting just six feet below me. I placed my hand on the ground positioning it right about where I imagined his hands rested. It was the closest I could get to Todd. My thoughts and emotions threatened to suffocate me. *"How could my baby be gone for the rest of my life? How was I supposed to live without him?"*

Despite the sadness in my heart, the day was beautiful, the sky a perfect blue with white, fluffy clouds. Todd's plot sits in the back of the cemetery, so no sounds from the nearby road reached me. The shade of a nearby tree perfectly covered Todd's plot. I was thankful for the location. Whenever I come to the cemetery, the Lord will allow me to be covered in shade.

For the first month or two after Todd's funeral, God's continual care for our family was visible in so many ways. The outpouring from friends, coworkers, and even strangers amazed us. We received hundreds of sympathy cards. People brought meals and gift cards. We even received a box of cookies from the Valastro family at Carlo's Bakery. They had spent only a few hours with our family, so it meant a lot that they cared enough to send us a reminder of their sympathy. We also received a card from Kelly Ripa and Michael Strahan, and one from their station manager. Our Shepherding Group continued to uphold us in any way they could. Several of Todd's doctors and nurses sent cards or texts; some even came to the funeral. Todd had touched many lives, not because he was popular or important in the community, but because in the midst of a devastating trial, he continued smiling and trusting in the Lord.

I thought the room makeover would end with Todd's death, and David and I would have to finish the work on our own. This was not the case. The week after Todd's funeral, Shannon contacted me about finishing the project. I was shocked. Later that week, he hung beautiful blinds and window treatments. When the decorations and new bedding came in, he put the finishing touches on the room. All the while, he checked with Jeffrey to make sure he liked everything. My favorite part of the remodel was the large picture of Todd and Jeffrey that Shannon hung on the wall. The picture was taken shortly after Todd's port placement surgery. Instead of the usual pose with Todd's arms wrapped protectively around Jeffrey, Jeffrey's arm circled protectively around Todd.

Through the first few months, I felt as though I was handling Todd's death fairly well, but then things began to change. After several months, cards no longer came in on a daily basis, people no longer brought meals, the grass grew in over Todd's grave, and for most people, life moved on. Each of us dealt with grief in our own way, and most of the time, as is common, our grief came at different times. David was busy with work and often didn't have time to just sit and reflect on our loss. Brandon, Lauren, and Jeffrey, were involved with school, and their lives had some sense of normalcy. My life did not move on, and there was nothing normal about it. For the most part, I spent the day alone—although Gracie was always at my feet. I was not working, and my days were no longer spent caring for Todd. I didn't know what to do with myself. Although I knew the Lord was with me, I no longer sensed His close presence the way I did while Todd was sick. I tried to remember the positive aspects of our journey, but at times, I felt myself slipping into a dark place. Evenings were difficult—especially Fridays at 9:20. I would watch the clock and think about what it must have been like for Todd to meet Jesus at that moment. Tears inevitably followed. I appreciated my family so much for their understanding of those moments. David or one of the kids would wrap their arms around me and let me cry. One week night as I was working at the computer, Jeffrey suddenly ran up and hugged me. I smiled at him and said, "What's that for?"

"Its 9:20."

My heart melted with love for Jeffrey and his tenderness toward me. From that day on, very often I receive what has become known as my "9:20 hug."

Writing Facebook posts sharing my honest feelings, yet remembering the blessings we had during Todd's cancer journey, helped me cope. I knew many people read my posts because they truly cared how our family was doing. For that reason, I made sure I didn't write anything too negative. People were watching our family to see how we dealt with losing our child, and I really did want to have the right attitude in dealing with my grief. No matter how hard I tried to remain positive, at times our loss overwhelmed me. I did not feel comfortable expressing these thoughts publicly, so I kept a journal detailing how I really felt.

> Nothing is the same after losing your child. He is not in his bed at night. He is not at the dinner table. He is not in his normal seat in the car. His clothes aren't in the wash. He is not sitting beside me at church. When David and the kids are in a room with me, someone is missing, and it does not feel right. I go to the car line to pick up my other kids after school and see Todd's friends running by me to soccer practice and I think, *"He should be running with them."* I find myself going into his closet just to smell his shirts hanging there on the top rung. I open his drawers, pull out a T-shirt, unfold it, and then refold it and put it away. I call his cell phone just to listen to his voice on the message. He spoke so fast that it is literally about five seconds long, but I still get to hear his voice, and for those five seconds, he is with me.
>
> Grief is suffocating! Sometimes I cry until I feel like I could throw up. At times, it feels as if I have a huge weight resting on my heart. Sometimes—many times—I want to die. I do not want to live with this pain for the rest of my life. Everyone seems fine. David goes to work as always. Brandon, Lauren, and Jeffrey go to school. They

all do what they normally do. Their lives go on. Hopefully, the kids will all marry and have their own families. My life will never, ever be the same.

I cannot understand why God puts such a powerful love in a mother's heart, but then He takes her child. How are we supposed to survive this kind of loss? If it were not for the Lord, I honestly believe I would be more than tempted to take my life. I may be able to survive the pain of losing my child if the pain of feeling like the Lord let me down didn't accompany it. I trusted Him. I brought my broken child to Him for healing, believing that God was the only One who could truly heal Todd, but when I placed Todd in His arms, He took my son and walked away. I can't explain the deep pain I feel because of that. How can I believe God still does miracles? I still love Him; I just don't know what to say to Him anymore.

Recently, people told me the verses I claimed about healing meant that God would heal Todd only if it was His will. Well, why doesn't it say that? The verses I claimed didn't say that God healed only if it was His will. The verses in Matthew 9:18–22 said He would heal. Now I don't know how to claim any Scripture at all. How I wish the Lord would just come for me and take me out of my misery.

I came home from a trip recently and Todd wasn't in the car with the family. He was not at home to greet me. I think of my precious boy lying in his casket in that cold ground. I would give anything to cover him with a blanket. I feel so bad that I didn't cover him. I wish I could hold him in my arms. I wish he could talk to me, and tell me he loves me and that I am doing a good job living without him even though I know I am not! I wish he could tell me what heaven is like. I want to know if I correctly explained what his death would be like. I would ask, "Todd, did you leave our couch and arrive in heaven in the blink of an eye? Was Jesus right there to meet you? Did you see someone who looked like Jeffrey? Were Uncle Bo and Grandpa there to meet you? Can't you please tell me something?

I want to know all about your mansion, Todd. Does it have a sweet tea spigot just for you? Do you have your own A.1. dispenser? Is my mansion being prepared for me right next door to yours? Are you helping the Lord design my mansion? Todd, remember how you used to draw your dream house all the time? Did the Lord incorporate any of your drawings into your mansion? I think that would be so neat.

Life is not all okay just because it was God's will to take your loved one. You suffer. God's grace is sufficient, but it does not take the pain away at all. My eyes look empty to me. I could not give someone a genuine smile if they paid me. I try to smile and be happy, but I don't hide my pain well. Will I ever find true joy in this lifetime?

As the New Year begins, my heart aches because Todd isn't in it. We won't make any family memories with him. New family pictures won't have him in them. I keep looking around the house for some sign of him. I miss my baby so much.

Had I known that Friday night would be my last night with Todd, I would have asked him if I could wrap him in a blanket and rock him in my arms one more time. In truth, had I known, I could never have let him go. I wonder if, as he fell asleep, he wanted me to sit in the living room with him but was too embarrassed to ask me.

> I should not have gone to bed that night. I didn't know it
> was our last night together.

Thankfully, the deep darkness I felt when I wrote those thoughts did not last for long, but a few concerns continued to plague me after Todd's death. For one thing, it bothered me that Todd didn't want to talk to Pastor Hoskinson when we were in New York City. I knew Todd's refusal had nothing to do with whether or not he liked him as a person, so I figured Todd didn't want to talk about dying. It also bothered me that Todd didn't feel the need to talk to his youth pastor, Abe. I thought for sure he would want to open up to Abe about his feelings, but this was not the case. After much discussion, I finally convinced Todd to let Pastor Abe come over and watch *Andy Griffith* with him. They did not have to talk about anything serious, I promised. At that, Todd agreed right away. They ate lunch and laughed while watching TV. When Abe started to leave, Todd asked him to stay for one more episode. Another time, when Pastor Danny wanted to visit, Todd only reluctantly agreed to let him come. Todd knew Pastor Danny his entire life and always enjoyed being around him, but he never opened up to Danny about how he felt emotionally or spiritually. Todd's reticence bothered me. I wanted someone to find out whether Todd knew he was dying and whether he was scared. In those last hours, Todd never said he could see heaven or angels or anything else I was told he might see or speak about. Although the Lord had given me peace on the night Todd died, once again I began to question whether he was really in heaven. One day I mentioned my concern to Kristen. In response, she wisely asked me two questions. "Did Todd ever give you any reason to believe he wasn't saved?"

Emphatically, I said, "No!"

She continued, "Did Todd ever give you any reason to believe he was saved?"

I could absolutely say, "Yes." Her questions helped to take away my fear. I remember listening to Todd when he was a child as he prayed and asked Jesus to forgive his sins and be his personal Savior. Todd's life showed me he was committed to his decision to follow Christ. Satan was clearly trying to torment me and convince me I needed signs to believe Todd was in heaven. Our conversation removed my fear about Todd's salvation once and for all, but I still could not figure out why he did not want to share his feelings with any of the pastors.

Two months after Todd died, my dear friend Aimee came to visit. As we talked, she wanted to give me the details of a conversation she had with Todd on an earlier visit—a conversation he had asked her not to share with me until after he died. Todd adored Aimee, and during that visit he asked for an opportunity to talk with her alone. Aimee related to Todd in a way the rest of us could not; she understood what he was going through. She survived a rare form of cancer and is a living miracle.

To give them privacy, the other kids and I left the house. When we returned, I pulled Aimee aside, asking anxiously, "What did you and Todd talk about?" I wanted answers to questions that I didn't know whether I should ask Todd myself.

Kindly, she answered, "We had a wonderful talk, but Todd asked me to keep it private." Her response disappointed me, but I respected Todd's wishes and didn't question her any further.

I had forgotten about their talk until she reminded me, so I drank in the words as she spoke.

Aimee recalled that Todd's first question to her was, "Do you know what it feels like to die?"

"I've felt like I was truly in the process of dying twice, Todd."

Todd continued, "I know I'm dying. I can feel the tumor growing inside me, and I know I don't have long to live. I'm not afraid of what it will be like after I die, because I know I'm going to heaven. I just don't know what it will feel like to actually die."

Aimee began to relay to me how she told Todd about the two instances where she actually thought she was in the process of dying and what that was like for her. As she spoke, her eyes filled with tears, and I could tell their conversation had been so tender, so private, and so special that I didn't want her to relive those sweet, yet painful, memories with me. I stopped her in the conversation and told her to let the discussion about dying remain between her and Todd. I knew whatever took place during that part of their conversation could be understood by only those two people. For in their conversation, heaven seemed more real to both of them than it has ever felt to me.

After Aimee answered Todd's question, she remarked to me that Todd's fears vanished. He was at peace about the nearness of his death. She then relayed to me that Todd's next statement seemed to trouble him.

"I wish people would stop asking me if I'm sure I'm saved. I don't think they understand how that question makes me feel. I feel like they must not be able to tell I'm a Christian or they just ask me because they want to make themselves feel better."

Todd knew his eternal security was settled when he trusted Jesus as His Savior as a young boy. After hearing that Todd felt this way, I thanked the Lord that He prevented me from asking Todd to tell me his salvation experience the night we had our special talk. At the time, I was disappointed in myself for not confirming his salvation experience just one more time. Todd was right. I just wanted to comfort myself with his words without thinking about the fact that I could see Jesus in him by the way he lived his life.

Finally, I knew why Todd did not feel the need to talk to any of the pastors about dying. His eternal security was already settled in his heart. He desired to talk with Aimee about death because he knew she would understand as no one else could. Aimee told me that it was Todd's desire with the little time he had remaining on this earth, to bring comfort to his family; he didn't want to spend time talking with everyone about death. Todd also confided in Aimee that he was worried about how I would handle his death. With great wisdom, Aimee responded, "Todd, you know the peace the Lord has given you through all of this?"

"Yes."

"That's the peace He will give your mom."

Todd told Aimee how much he loved David and me and his brothers and sister. Listening to Aimee recount this part of their conversation was a wonderful gift. Although he was the one dying, Todd was thinking about others—another evidence of God's grace in his life. Finally, I had the answers to the questions that troubled me. He knew he was dying, and he was not afraid.

About five months after Todd passed away, I lay in bed one night sobbing until I could not breathe. I begged God, *"Please let me hug Todd in my dreams."* In the early hours of the morning, God granted my prayer. In my dream I sat in the car watching Todd, healthy and whole, a little boy with that huge, wonderful smile. Through the open window, I asked him to come close to me and put his cheek next to mine. I stroked his face, telling him that I loved him and missed him so much. Abruptly, I woke, sobbing happy tears for the moments we were together and sad tears because, once again, Todd was gone. Months later, I had a similar dream, but this time Todd was a grinning teenager dressed in the puffy black coat he often wore. I asked if I could hug him, and he gathered me in his arms. Waking up from such a precious moment was painful, but I thanked God for Todd's hugs, even if they were only in my dreams.

Brenda Lurtey

Chapter 37

The Gift of Time

A friend once reminded me that a drowning person cannot be saved until he stops thrashing. I wondered whether that was how God viewed me. He wanted to throw me a lifeline all along, but He waited to reveal some of His promises to me until I was ready to stop fighting and be still before Him.

One day at Todd's grave, I dropped to my knees and began sobbing. I begged, *"Lord, why did you heal Todd in Charleston if you were just going to take him away?"* That brief period of joy now seemed like a bitter tease.

Immediately, I heard His voice gently speak to my heart.

"To give you time."

I stopped crying and lifted my head with the reality of His words. The Lord had my attention.

"Thank you, Lord," I prayed with bowed head. *"We did have the gift of time."*

I thought back to all the pictures we took, all the conversations we shared, all the memories we made, and I was overwhelmed with thankfulness. I said, "I love you"—all I could possibly say. I had memorized Todd's features and held his hand, and he was sweet enough to let me. I like to think God spoke to his heart and prepared him for what was ahead—including the realization that his mother would need to say her earthly goodbyes to him. Todd listened patiently and attentively as I shared my heart with him the night before he died. I believe God actually readied Todd for death years ago when Todd told me he might die early. I do not know what else would have prompted him to say such a thing except the Lord's desire to prepare him for that journey.

When I viewed Todd's death from a different perspective, I knew it was time to listen to what the Lord wanted to teach me. Submitting was a long process. I was no longer angry at Him for taking Todd, but I still did not fully understand why He did.

As life continued, I tried to make it meaningful instead of wallowing in my sorrow. The first Thanksgiving after Todd's death, we decided to visit some of David's relatives. Getting out of town helped us deal with painful memories. Just twelve months earlier, Todd had had his life-saving surgery in Charleston. He was supposed to lead a full and healthy life afterward, but he did not, and the knowledge of our loss dominated our minds. As I busied myself with meal preparations, I reminded myself that the Lord could have taken Todd during, or even before, that surgery. Instead, the Lord chose to give us more time together. I tried to have a heart full of thankfulness for the gift of time we had with Todd, rather than dwelling on our loss.

Christmas without Todd was difficult; yet David and I wanted to honor him without filling the day with sadness for us and Brandon, Lauren, and Jeffrey. After breakfast, we placed fresh flowers on and took pictures around Todd's grave. Later we delivered cupcakes and gifts to the patients and nurses on the fifth floor of the hospital. After spending holidays there, we knew what it felt like to be away from home. Returning was bittersweet, but reaching out to others in need blessed us.

After a sweet time in the hospital, we spent the rest of the day with my parents, my sister, and her family. We all gave and received special gifts that reflected our relationships with Todd. We gave my parents a woven blanket with a picture of all ten of their grandchildren. Brandon, Lauren, and Jeffrey each received a printed blanket with a photo of all four siblings that our friend Christa had taken in March before Todd died. To this day, they proudly display the blankets on their beds.

We shed tears for Todd, but our grief did not define the day. Instead, we did our best to honor Todd and remember what we were really celebrating: the birth of Jesus Christ. Although the day had sad moments, overall it was precious.

The thought of Todd in heaven on his birthday made me happy for him, but it was difficult for me, especially since we always shared our birthdays. In spite of my sadness, I decided to remember Todd with a birthday party his classmates, now sophomores, could attend. I bought two cakes, each decorated with his picture and the words, "Happy 1st Birthday in Heaven." One of the kids asked that they all sing "In Christ Alone," the last song Todd sang when his youth group came to our house. Hearing his friends sing this song brought me to tears.

After the party, I took fresh flowers and the balloons from the party to Todd's grave. I could hardly believe I had to celebrate my precious son's birthday at his graveside, but I made his grave look as pretty as possible. Todd's birthday was the best day we could have possibly made it. Although we cried at times, I felt we did something positive with our grief, and I hoped we celebrated Todd's memory through it all.

Brenda Lurtey

Chapter 38

Lessons from Lazarus

With every blessing the Lord gives us, Satan is quick to whisper his lies in our ears. Even though the Lord showed me His love by giving us the gift of more time with Todd, I still allowed Satan to make me question how a God who supposedly loved me could cause me such pain.

During Todd's illness, I read John 11—the story of Jesus raising Lazarus from the dead—repeatedly, claimed it when I prayed for Todd's healing, and read it even more after he died. This passage confused me. I could not understand why Jesus did not come when He knew Lazarus was sick and why He wept just moments before He raised Lazarus from the dead. Why, I wondered, did Jesus heal Lazarus but not Todd? Did I not have enough faith? Sometimes reading the Bible was difficult. Nothing made sense.

Although I gradually felt better than I had in the first few weeks after Todd died, I was still in a bad place emotionally and spiritually. Before he died, I promised Todd that if the time ever came when I was not okay, I would get help. Eventually, I realized I needed to make good on that promise, but I was not sure where to turn. Who would truly understand my struggles?

One day, David told me Pastor Will, a visiting pastor who was in the second group that prayed over Todd at church, wanted to talk to us. We didn't have much time to talk, so I quickly fired question after question at him. He answered some of them before suggesting I read the book *Praying Backwards* by Bryan Chapell. I love to read, and I wanted answers, so I gratefully took down the information. I asked Pastor Will a few more questions. With each one, he smiled and said, "Read that book. It will answer your questions." I purchased it that night. The book changed my life and gave me a completely new perspective on God.

While reading the book, the first truth that struck me was how I limited God by telling Him how I thought Todd's life story should play out, as if He needed my input to accomplish His will. This sentence from the book struck me: "Prayer does not relieve all suffering, but it assures us that no difficulty comes without a purpose" (12). I knew I had been dead wrong in my approach to Todd's illness. Subconsciously, I thought as a follower of Jesus Christ, I should be exempt from suffering. Unfortunately, the curse of sin made pain and suffering an integral part of this world. Jesus suffered immensely on this earth because of sin's curse.

A major theme of *Praying Backwards* is that we should pray for everything in the name of Jesus, relying on His wisdom in choosing to answer our requests. God is not my personal genie, waiting around to grant my wishes. I needed to petition God first and foremost that His will be accomplished. Focusing on His will shifts the focus off our selfish desires. Bryan Chapell notes, "Praying backwards is an attitude of the heart (22)." And later he says, "When we pray in Jesus's name, He will give us the desire of our heart because our heart's greatest joy will be for His will to be done" (25).

Of course, God's decision not to heal Todd on this earth disappointed me, but as I read this book, the Scriptures came alive. I will never know why the Lord took Todd home to heaven when He did, but I began to trust that God fulfilled a greater purpose in Todd's death than through his healing. Matthew 26:39 records Christ's prayer in the Garden of Gethsemane: "My Father, if it be possible, let this cup pass from me; nevertheless, not as I will, but as you will." Jesus prayed for deliverance, but submitted to the will of His Father.

As I continued reading, these words stood out: "Our prayers will always be limited by human knowledge and vision. Yet God acts sovereignly. He knows the future we cannot discern and infinite consequences we cannot anticipate" (55). I wondered whether the agony of losing my son to cancer would pale in comparison to the agony I would have experienced had Todd lived, only to walk away from the Lord one day. I have no reason to believe Todd would have rejected Him, but I cannot know for sure. Perhaps the Lord took Todd to protect him from a future hurt I could not see. My human reasoning is fallible, and it is not my place to figure out God's motivation. I have to trust that the Lord did what was best for Todd.

The Lord worked on my faith. Would I still trust and love Him when I could not understand what He was doing on Todd's behalf? As Bryan Chapell noted, "The heart of faith believes what the eye cannot observe of God's hand" (77). I had cried out to the Lord, reminding Him of all the times He granted requests for healing, but He did not seem to answer mine. Gradually, I realized this was not the case. He did answer my prayers. The Bible tells us Paul asked the Lord to remove a thorn in his flesh three times, yet He did not remove it. He reminded Paul in 2 Corinthians 12:9, "My grace is sufficient for you, for my power is made perfect in weakness." The Lord did not remove Paul's trial, but He gave Paul strength to endure his trial. The same was true for me and my family.

The final quote from *Praying Backwards* that touched my heart was this: "God alone knows whether Christ will receive more glory through the removal of our trial, through the continued faithfulness in the midst of suffering, or through an ultimate sacrifice that takes us to heaven where pain is replaced by eternal praise of unending joy" (101). How could I possibly argue that my way was best? I couldn't. The issue boiled down to whether I was going to submit to the infinite wisdom of God or keep using my human reasoning to figure out what was going on. I realized I had to choose to trust Him even when I could not see His purpose.

Shortly before Todd died, Pastor Danny began preaching a series of messages on the book of John in our Sunday evening services. I could not wait for him to get to John 11. No matter how I tried, I couldn't wrap my mind around that chapter. Several months after Todd's death, the Sunday evening finally arrived when Pastor Danny preached from John 11. As he spoke, I sat in the service with tears streaming down my cheeks. I felt as though a veil was being lifted from blind eyes. I began to understand the passage for the first time in my life.

First of all, I understood that although Jesus raised Lazarus from the dead, it was only temporary—Lazarus did die again at some point. However, I did not understand why Jesus chose to give him life for another period of time. I emailed Pastor Danny asking for more clarification. To answer my "why" question, Pastor Danny asked me to read John 11:4. The verse says, "This illness does not lead to death. **It is for the glory of God,** so that the Son of God may be glorified through it." As Danny later pointed out in his email, John 11:26 says, "And everyone who lives and believes in me shall never die. Do you believe this?" He went on to instruct me that although Lazarus and Todd and even Danny's own mother had died, because each had placed faith in Jesus, they never ceased to exist. They passed from this world into eternal life in heaven. Death is a passing over. I understood what he was telling me, and I saw Todd's death from a new perspective.

Next, Pastor Danny pointed me to John 11:38–44: "Then Jesus, deeply moved again, came to the tomb [where Lazarus was buried]. It was a cave, and a stone lay against it. Jesus said, 'Take away the stone.' Martha, the sister of the dead man, said to him, 'Lord, by this time there will be an odor, for he has been dead four days.' Jesus said to her, 'Did I not tell you that if you believed you would see the glory of God?' So they took away the stone. And Jesus lifted up his eyes and said, 'Father, I thank you that you have heard me. I knew that you always hear me, but I said this on account of the people standing around, that they may believe that you sent me.' When he had said these things, he cried out with a loud voice, 'Lazarus, come out.' The man who had died came out, his hands and feet bound with linen strips, and his face wrapped with a cloth. Jesus said to them, 'Unbind him, and let him go.'" Jesus' friends saw a miracle performed right before their eyes—Jesus raised a man that had been dead for four days.

There was something else that troubled me from John 11. Even though Jesus raised Lazarus from the dead, I didn't understand why, when Jesus heard that His friend Lazarus was sick, He waited for two days before making the trip back to Bethany. In my human reasoning, I knew that if a friend needed me, I would go to that person right away. I wondered whether Jesus delayed His return because He knew that His friends needed a visual sign that He is the resurrection and the life—maybe they needed to actually view His power.

After Jesus returned to Bethany, He spoke with Martha. In John 11:23 Jesus said, "Your brother will rise again." Martha replied in John 11:24,

"I know he will rise again in the resurrection on the last day." In the next verse Jesus said to her, "**I am** the resurrection and the life. Whoever believes in me, though he die, yet shall he live, and everyone who lives and believes in me shall <u>never</u> die. Do you believe this?"

Pastor Danny explained to me, "Jesus came to put our lives in perspective. And one of the things He is continually doing during His ministry is demonstrating that <u>what we believe are the greatest realities</u> (the greatest "glories") are <u>not</u> the greatest realities. **HE** is the greatest reality, the greatest glory. So He actually waits to make the one-day journey back to Bethany until after Lazarus has died so that He can show Martha, Mary, the mourners, and his disciples that He is awesome in His glory; more awesome than death itself." I finally understood the passage of Scripture as Danny explained it to me and it comforted me to know that Jesus had a divine purpose in mind for allowing His friends to suffer the grief of their brother's death.

I asked further, "Was His delay also because He felt that His friends needed a 'sign' that He is the resurrection and the life? It seems that in John 11:25, when He asked Martha whether she believed, her answer ('Yes, Lord; I believe that you are the Christ, the Son of God, who is coming into the world') wasn't the point He was trying to make."

Pastor Danny replied,

Martha is giving Jesus the right theological answer: "Yes, I believe in a resurrection to come." Jesus wants her and us to see that our theology is tied so closely to a Person. It is more precise and accurate to say, "We believe that Jesus <u>is</u> the Resurrection and the Life." It's the difference between saying, "I know a lady named Brenda Lurtey exists" and saying "I know Brenda Lurtey exists because she is my friend." We know that there is a resurrection to come and that there is a real spiritual life to be lived now because we know the One who <u>is</u> the Resurrection and the Life. Imagine how that experience with the Lord transformed Martha, Mary, Lazarus, the disciples, and others! They got a little foretaste of the great resurrection to come. They watched the God/Man do the thing that they already believed He could and would do—such an intensely personal privilege for them. And having the first-person account from the book of John is a privilege for us! This is really great stuff. It's like the family history that gets passed from one generation to the next, only this isn't made up and it hasn't been embellished. The God we believe in actually did this for Lazarus. The God we're banking our hope in stood at the tomb of a dead family member and wept! And then He called him out of that tomb. And He will do it for us!

I continued to be comforted as I let the truth of Scripture as explained to me by my pastor sink into my heart. The last part of John 11 that really baffled me was why Jesus cried at the tomb of Lazarus when He knew He was about to raise Lazarus from the dead. Pastor Danny answered that question in his sermon that Sunday evening, but reiterated it in his email to me.

Brenda, do you think Jesus shared your grief as you said goodbye to Todd? I do. I absolutely do. I think Jesus still weeps with us because His love for us is so intense. The proof is in this story (of Lazarus) of shared grief and tears. I think He still roars in His spirit as He watches sin and death take their toll on the world He created. I love that about Him. I love having such a personal God and Savior. I love having a Savior who is still flesh and blood, who remembers what it was like to wake up in the morning and have to scrounge up some breakfast, to feel His stomach churn when viruses were going around, to struggle with His earthly family through the grief of losing their dad, to feel the pain of rejection and misunderstanding even though He was doing exactly what His God and Father called Him to do. He's fully human. And sorrow is a part of the human experience.

After hearing Pastor Danny's sermon on John 11 and reading his email comments, I finally understood why Jesus wept. He looked around at the people He loved and saw the grief they suffered because sin brought death into the world. John 11:35 is not just the shortest verse in the Bible; it is a profound statement that shows that Jesus deeply feels our pain more than we will ever know. I realized the Lord did not take pleasure in taking Todd away from me, causing this deep ache in my heart. In His infinite wisdom, He knew Todd's death—and not his healing—is what would ultimately bring Him glory. Although He did what was best for Todd and our family and everyone who loved Todd, He still shared in our sorrow. To know Jesus shared in my sorrow was overwhelming. Furthermore, I realized Lazarus's resurrection was only temporary. He eventually did die again one day. Even if the Lord had chosen to heal Todd of his cancer, he would have eventually died one day too. Death is a curse of sin—something none of us are exempt from, but because Jesus died for the sins of Lazarus and for the sins of Todd, they both live in heaven today. Jesus died for the sins of the whole world. We all can have the joy of living in heaven one day if we accept His free gift of eternal life.

Throughout Todd's illness, I wanted visible proof that the Lord is who He says He is. I asked to see a miracle—but I wanted His power displayed on my terms. I wanted to be in charge of the game plan, I wanted to be the author of Todd's story, and I wanted to control how things would play out.

The Lord said no to the miracle of healing I asked for, but He did display His love and power to me in visible ways. Friends and strangers, by their acts of kindness on behalf of our family, became like the hands and feet of Jesus. They shared our burdens and showed us love along the way. The Lord used the expertise and care of Todd's doctors to comfort him during his cancer journey; and in comforting him, they comforted David and me. One of the greatest things the Lord did for Todd was to put His hand on Todd's pain. The malignant peripheral nerve sheath tumor should have caused Todd to die in agony, but it did not. In his last days, the tumor could have confined him to a hospital bed, but it did not. He could have spent his last days in a coma, but he did not. He could have suffered the humiliation of losing control of bodily functions, but he did not. We could have resorted to begging God to take Todd's life because of prolonged pain, but we did not. The Lord took Todd home quickly and peacefully, just as I had asked Him to do. Seeing firsthand how the Lord watched over my son makes me very thankful. It was a gift.

In the end, the Lord ministered to me each step of the way. When sadness overwhelmed me, He provided a verse of comfort or sent someone to give me a hug or offer a word of kindness and encouragement. He continues to do so to this day.

Am I still a little disappointed in God? Honestly? Maybe a little bit, but I am truly learning—and it is a process—that He is who He says He is. He is good all the time, even if I do not agree with His plans for my life. I know He loves me more than I will ever realize. How do I know this? His Word says this is true. I should not be disappointed with God when He does not do what I want Him to do. He never promises to fulfill my agenda, but He does promise to be true to His Word.

Do I still miss Todd? Yes, and I always will in this lifetime! Do I still cry for him? Oh, yes, and I am sure I will cry many tears until I am finally reunited with Todd one day! As the Scriptures say in 1 Thessalonians 4:13, "But we do not want you to be uninformed, brothers, about those who are asleep, that you may not grieve as others who have no hope." I remind myself of this verse all the time. If Todd's life ended at the grave, I would have every reason in the world to despair, but it did not end at the grave. At 9:20 p.m. on Friday, May 10, 2013, Todd's life had truly just begun.

The Lord's eyes saw everything that took place in Todd's life from the moment he was formed in my womb, through his childhood, his NF1 diagnosis, his cancer diagnosis, and his homegoing. When I did not have a clue what He was doing, His eyes saw what was going on in our lives, and He had everything under control. His eyes saw not only my emotional needs but also my spiritual needs. He is still meeting these needs one day at a time.

The Lord's eyes saw every single person that prayed for our family. Our request for prayer was passed from friends and family until people all over the world were praying for Todd's healing. The Lord's eyes saw them all. Yet, in His wisdom, He said no to each of our requests—at least here on earth. He did heal Todd, but that healing took place in Glory. The answer to my "Why, Lord?" question is found in John 11:4. "But when Jesus heard it he said, "This illness does not lead to death. It is for the glory of God, so that the Son of God may be glorified through it." This is all the Lord has chosen to reveal to me and this is where my faith and human reasoning collide. Human reasoning demands a sign to believe something is true; faith takes God at His Word. Every day I have to make the conscious choice to trust the Lord even when I do not understand. He has a master plan, and it is perfect.

Todd is my hero. He suffered and died with a dignity I could only hope to mirror. Todd did not suffer and die graciously because of who he is, but because of who Jesus is. Psalm 23 says, "Even though I walk through the valley of the shadow of death, I will fear no evil, for you are with me." Todd did not walk through that valley alone. Jesus walked with him, just as He promised He would. When Todd's journey was finally over, I believe Jesus reached for his hand, maybe just as Todd gently rubbed his thumbs over mine for the last time, and then led him through the gates of Paradise. Todd's life on earth ended on May 10, 2013, but his life in heaven was just beginning.

To my precious son Todd:

You were right. The Lord did take you to heaven while you were young, and there was nothing I could do about it. He was so kind and gracious to prepare you for your death so long ago, and the peace He gave you was amazing. I cannot begin to express how much I miss you. A piece of my heart will always be with you, but I am so thankful you are safe and healthy and are enjoying all the wonders of heaven. You are my hero, and I am honored that the Lord allowed me to be your mom. The sixteen years He gave us together were wonderful, and I will always treasure them.

I'm so proud of the way you lived and even how you died. I consider it a great privilege that the Lord allowed me to walk with you through your journey, and I can't wait to join you in heaven one day. After I spend a long time in the arms of the Lord, I want to look up and see your smile. When I do, I'll run into your arms. Meet me at heaven's gate!

Until then, all my love,

Mom

Afterword

The day the Lord spoke to my heart and showed me His kindness in giving us the gift of time, I began to move forward in my journey of grief. Although I still have many hard times, the Lord has taught me and continues to teach me numerous positive lessons. As I recalled the many acts of kindness people bestowed on our family during Todd's illness and even after his home going, my heart was filled with gratitude. So many people provided gifts or used their unique talents to bless our family. God knew what we needed, and He always laid it on the hearts of those best suited to answer those needs. One of my favorite passages is Matthew 25:34-40:

> "Come, you who are blessed by my Father, inherit the kingdom prepared for you from the foundation of the world. For I was hungry and you gave me food, I was thirsty and you gave me drink, I was a stranger and you welcomed me, I was naked and you clothed me, I was sick and you visited me, I was in prison and you came to me." Then the righteous will answer him, saying, "Lord, when did we see you hungry and feed you, or thirsty and give you drink? And when did we see you a stranger and welcome you, or naked and clothe you? And when did we see you sick or in prison and visit you?" And the King will answer them, "Truly, I say to you, as you did it to one of the least of these my brothers, you did it to me."

The countless cups of cold water given in the name of the Lord have forever changed our family. My purpose in sharing our blessings is not to brag, but rather to provide ideas for others to use to bless their neighbors in their time of need. I pray that God will bless every stranger or friend who ministered to our family during our greatest time of need.

Brenda Lurtey

Appendix

Blessings

In the midst of heartache, the Lord brought great joy into our lives. He worked in many ways and used different people—strangers and friends—to bring Todd happiness and to walk with us through our difficult journey.

Bob had an amazing car he affectionately called "The Chief." The 1940 Pontiac was so shiny and smooth that it practically begged admirers to run their fingers along its sleek side. Bob strongly discouraged anyone from touching The Chief; greasy fingerprints were absolutely not allowed! One weekend, Bob and his wife Joann invited Todd to attend a car show with them. As hard as it was for me to let Todd out of my sight, I wanted him to have fun, so I agreed to let him go. I worried he might get too tired, and I did not want Bob and Joann to stay in the hotel room instead of getting out at night, so I asked David to go along. They had a wonderful time. Todd rode in style to Charlotte, North Carolina, in The Chief and then checked out all the other cars at the show. The next day, they visited the Charlotte Motor Speedway and the Panther's Stadium. Todd loved the Panthers, so visiting the stadium was a special treat.

Terri paid for me to have Todd's thumbprint cast in a silver necklace. Todd and I went to the artist's studio where she made a mold of his thumbprint and then filled it with silver. While she worked, she asked why we were having the jewelry made. She listened intently while I shared some of Todd's story with her. When we left, she gave Todd what I am sure was the biggest and longest hug he ever received from a stranger. Her interaction with Todd was so compassionate and genuine.

Sadly, that was the first and last time they ever met. To this day, I treasure that necklace and the precious memories we made.

Our Sunday School class gave our family a binder full of restaurant gift cards. This generous gesture made our lives much easier. Todd's illness made routine tasks like shopping and cleaning hard to even think about. The cards to restaurants our family enjoyed took the pressure off all of us to purchase and prepare food.

Although most family suppers were supplied by friends or by using the gift cards, school lunches had to be prepared daily. Since I was usually at the hospital, Lauren was in charge of making them. Jenny provided a variety of nutritious lunch items that were a wonderful help to Lauren.

While I was in the hospital with Todd, Leah delivered a huge box filled with granola bars, applesauce, desserts, crackers, and other food items. She even gave me a single-serve coffee machine. The food box was a blessing. I never wanted to leave Todd for very long to go to the hospital cafeteria, and sometimes I just didn't want much to eat. Not only did Leah give me a supply of food to enjoy in the hospital room, but she also came to visit several times and brought pizza or other hot foods.

I did not have time to shop for Christmas presents, let alone decorate. When I came home to arrangements of pine boughs, wreaths, and ornaments on the door and front light post, I felt loved by our friends Jeff and Kim, who used their impressive talents to encourage our family during a difficult time in our lives.

Since Todd's needs consumed David and me, we worried Brandon, Lauren, and Jeffrey would feel neglected. Friends repeatedly invited them to do things with their families. Knowing my other kids were out having fun and not stuck at home helped me focus on taking care of Todd.

School let out before David got off work, so we needed someone to pick up the kids. Friends were always willing to help, and their kindness was a blessing to David and me.

With an extended illness come seemingly insurmountable medical bills. Thankfully, God moved many people to send monetary gifts of all sizes. Five or ten dollars may seem too tiny an amount to send someone in need, but those small bills added up to a huge help. When we realized the extent of Todd's disease, I quit my job to devote my time to his care. The money coming in to make up for my lost paycheck was a major blessing. We also received gas cards, which were wonderful, since David constantly drove between our house and the hospital.

Two local massage therapists gave Todd massages on several occasions. Their kindness brought tears to my eyes because it relieved Todd's pain, if only for a short time.

One sweet neighbor and friend offered to walk our dog. Gracie was just a puppy at the time of Todd's illness, and it was hard to suppress her energy—especially around Todd. Debbie helped our dog get rid of some of that energy, and it was a tremendous help.

I never realized how important family photos would be. Thinking about the future in the middle of fighting a life-threatening illness is difficult. Thankfully, Christa knew what the photos would mean to us. She took beautiful pictures of our family that we used at Todd's viewing and funeral and that are now scattered all over our house. We treasure them and the love she showed by taking them.

Jenny is a talented decorator. For Todd's viewing and funeral, she set up displays of items that represented Todd, accompanied by creative cards explaining what each thing meant to him. I was so proud of what she did for our family.

Diane and Lois prepared a delicious meal for our family on the night of the viewing. Another friend stayed in our house while we were gone just to be sure our home was safe.

After Todd died, numerous friends brought paper products, especially tissues! They also provided food, drinks, and snacks for all the family that came into town.

Our first family trip without Todd was difficult, but we had a wonderful, relaxing time at the beach timeshare Joan and Glenn gave us. Brandon, Lauren, and Jeffrey endured so much without the full attention of their parents. The beach trip allowed us to focus solely on them for the first time in a long time.

Many people sent us books that meant something to them during difficult times in their lives. I appreciated the books, not only because I love to read but also because someone took the time to reflect on what might benefit us most as we grieved. Everyone handles loss differently, but when those who have already been through that trial pass along something they found helpful, it is particularly meaningful.

Dan wrote a special song in Todd's honor. I was moved to think that while I might have been crying on my bed one night, he was thinking about the words that would bring comfort to our family. That took a tremendous amount of time, care, and concern.

Violet wrote out, laminated, and sent me the words to Lamentations 3:32: "But though He cause grief, he will have compassion according to the abundance of his steadfast love." This particular verse consoled her after she lost her brother to cancer several years prior to Todd's death, and now it consoles me.

When friends visit Todd's grave, they often tell me about it. This proves people have not forgotten our son; he is still loved. Recently, I found a single, long-stemmed rose lying on Todd's grave. I have no idea where it came from, but it is a special and tangible reminder that someone was thinking of him.

Rynda sent cards every month, and Ruth sent verses every week for the first year. Sending mail that often is not cheap, and it also takes effort. I appreciated the recognition that, although life was going on as normal for most people, they remembered my life would never be the same.

At Christmas, family friends (affectionately known as "MeMe and Papa") who send our family Christmas presents every year, included one in Todd's memory. I was so thankful he was not left out of our celebration.

Leaving the house and finding a new normal is hard, but important. Staying home and not facing people is a great temptation, but it can be detrimental to the healing process. Friends and laughter are necessary in life once again, so I took my friends up on their many lunch invitations. Todd would not have wanted me to isolate myself.

Just washing the dishes or doing the laundry was overwhelming during Todd's illness and in the aftermath of his death. Some days I gave myself permission to accomplish just one task. The prospect of cleaning the whole house was just too daunting. Some church friends offered their services to clean our house when Todd was sick, but knowing they worked hard for no pay made accepting difficult. After Todd died, Becca paid for a cleaning service several times. Agreeing was easier when I knew the cleaner was being paid. Either way, both gestures answered a true need.

Jim, a landscaper from our Sunday School class, made us a memory garden in our back yard full of plants from Todd's funeral. I absolutely love it. In addition to all the plants, the garden, complete with a waterfall, has a cement bench decorated with a hummingbird and a stepping-stone that reads, "When the loved one becomes a memory, the memory becomes a treasure." The garden is peaceful to look at, and I can add to it as the years go by.

Mark and his son Joseph, a long-time friend of Todd's, built a deck off the back of our house in memory of Todd. I love it, but I love the friendship we have with Mark and his family even more. Whenever I sit outside, I remember the hard work and kindness that went into this project. The deck gives us a perfect view of the memory garden.

What about you? What can you do for someone in need? It may be something from the list above or something else you have the ability to do. Maybe you can rake leaves, fix cars, or trim bushes. Most people want to help, but if you tell a family to give you a call if they need something, you will probably never hear from them unless they are very close friends. If you really want to help, it is best just to tell the family what the Lord has laid on your heart to do for them, and then do it!

Brenda Lurtey

Tough Adjustments

Please do not make the mistake of telling someone who has lost a child that you know exactly how he or she feels. You cannot possibly know exactly how he or she is feeling unless you have buried your own child. Also, please remember that we all respond to grief in different ways. The Lord made each one of us a unique individual. While you may look at someone who is grieving and think, "If it were me, I would do this or that"; you never truly know how you would respond unless the Lord gives you the same trial. Some people may think we should accept death and quickly move on, but our lives will never be the same. We do have to continue to live our lives, but moving forward in our new normal is a process and not one that happens quickly. I have listed a few things that have been especially hard for our family, not to obtain pity, but to give some insight as to why we, and other families who have lost a child/sibling, may have a hard time finding joy in our new normal.

Seeing the empty bed where your child once slept is very difficult. Jeffrey, who shared a room with Todd, now faces terrible loneliness and grief.

Our children usually sat with me in church since David always worked with the sound system. Todd's empty place is a constant reminder of our loss. In addition, looking toward the front of the church without visualizing the casket that held his body is nearly impossible.

Whenever we drove somewhere in our van, Brandon and Todd usually sat in the second row, and Lauren and Jeffrey sat in the third row. Our first family trip without Todd was extremely difficult. Lauren and Jeffrey chatted away in the third row; seeing Brandon beside Todd's empty seat just felt wrong. My heart ached not only for our loss as a family but also for Brandon's loss of his brother and friend.

Believe it or not, giving a waitress the number of people in our party can bring on the tears. Before Todd's death, we were a party of six; saying "just five" is too hard. When I am asked, I now respond, "There will be five of us tonight."

We never leave Todd's name out of a conversation about family events or activities. When David and I discuss where everyone will be for the day or evening, we include the fact that Todd is in heaven. He is still part of all we do with our family.

Seeing Todd's classmates walking to classes or sports activities together is difficult. I look at the soccer field and picture him playing with his friends. I enjoy seeing his friends; I just miss seeing Todd with all of them.

It is very hard to picture a future without your child in it. I do not have the strength today to think what it will be like to see Todd's friends—some he has known since infancy—graduate without him. I will never have the joy of having Todd walk me down the aisle before he marries the love of his life. Thinking of a future without Todd is sad, but God promises me strength only for today. When I am overwhelmed, I remind myself of Matthew 6:34, "Therefore, do not be anxious about tomorrow" and 2 Corinthians 12:9, "My grace is sufficient for you." The Lord does not promise to take away all our pain, but He promises grace to get us through.

Nearly every parent who has lost a child is tormented by different thoughts. If you know someone who has suffered that kind of loss, you can be assured that they have just come through a fierce battle for their child's life. I absolutely questioned myself. *"Should we have done more chemo? Should we have tried another surgery? If only I had tried this."* None of us want to wonder about whether or not our child was afraid to die. Parents are supposed to protect their children from fear and pain. These thoughts definitely tormented me at times, but none of us can stop death from happening. I felt as though I had let Todd down because I could not save his life. I am his mom. I was supposed to protect him.

People who do not respond to our child's death or to our needs as we think they should may become targets of our anger. If you are a dear friend, keep being one. Be available for your grieving friends if they want to talk. Unless you know a person well, try not to frequently ask, "How are you doing?" The question may come from a sincere heart, but that same question from multiple people can be frustrating. A grieving parent is not necessarily going to want to share his or her deepest feelings with just anyone. I appreciated it the most when people I did not know well told me they were still praying for our family but did not wait for me to respond with more than a thank you. Sometimes, just coming to church was hard enough; sharing my feelings with someone I did not know well was excruciating.

Emotions may run from one extreme to the other in a matter of minutes. I experienced this more than once. One day, I was fine, but when one of the kids just mentioned the word gravy, I started to cry. Todd loved gravy, and I knew I would never make gravy for him again. Another day, I saw a mother hugging her baby boy and kissing his cheeks. Tears welled in my eyes as I thought about kissing Todd goodbye for the last time. Sometimes memories bring smiles, and sometimes they bring tears—it just depends.

Through all of the tough adjustments, I am reminded that it is okay to cry. The Lord gave us tears for a reason, and one day He will personally wipe away our tears. Revelation 21:4 says, "He will wipe away every tear from their eyes, and death shall be no more, neither shall there be mourning, nor crying, nor pain anymore, for the former things have passed away." I look forward to that day with all my heart.

Brenda Lurtey

Positive Things to Do With Grief

Write about your experiences—people who care about you want to know how you are coping. They may not feel comfortable calling or asking all the time—especially if they are not close friends. I found the Facebook page created and maintained by a friend was the best way to let people know how Todd was doing throughout his illness. After his death, it was a way to inform people about how they could specifically pray for our family. Journaling my feelings helped me express myself during difficult times, but it also helped me to focus on the positive aspects of what the Lord has done for our family. I posted sad things, but I always tried to add something encouraging as well.

After a loved one dies, if possible, join a support group. People who have experienced similar circumstances know your pain, and you can encourage each other. Some people join support groups that do not address their particular needs. For example, I went to a cancer support group just a few weeks after Todd died. Unbeknown to me, the women in that group were all widows. I was the only lady who had lost a child. Thankfully, the leader suggested I might feel more comfortable with people who had lost a child to cancer. She was right. Our new group was the perfect fit for our family, and we have grown to love the members. We support each other on difficult anniversary dates—diagnosis of the child's illness, death of the child, the child's birthday—through texts, phone calls, or lunch dates.

Remember to do for others what others have done for you—or what you wish had been done for you. I will never forget the kindness others showed to us during Todd's illness and death, and now, I have plenty of ideas to help when someone I know loses a loved one.

When a difficult anniversary comes, instead of isolating yourself in the house, do something tangible to remember your child. Visit the hospital and bring treats to the patients, doctors, and nurses. You have a unique understanding of the fear the patients and parents are experiencing.

Helping others honors your child's life. You cannot buy your loved one a birthday or Christmas present, but you can buy a gift in your child's memory, or pay for another child to go to summer camp.

Second Corinthians 1:3 says, "Blessed be the God and Father of our Lord Jesus Christ, the Father of mercies and God of all comfort, who comforts us in all our affliction, so that we may be able to comfort those who are in any affliction, with the comfort with which we ourselves are comforted by God."

God bless each and every person who prayed for our family and helped us bear our burdens. We will never forget your kindness.

Works Cited

Chapell, Bryan. *Praying Backwards: Transform Your Prayer Life by Beginning in Jesus' Name.* Grand Rapids: Baker Publishing Group, 2005. Ebook edition, 2012. Web. 21 January 2016.

Courtney, Craig. "Be Not Afraid." Lyrics. Beckenhorst Press, Inc., 1992.

Cowman, L. B. *Streams in the Desert.* Ed. Jim Reimann. Grands Rapids: Zondervan, 1997. Print.

Getty, Keith, and Stuart Townend. "In Christ Alone." Lyrics. Kingsway Thankyou Music, 2001.

Mayo Foundation for Medical Education and Research. "Definition of Malignant Peripheral Nerve Sheath Tumors." *MayoClinic.org.* n.d. Web. 26 January 2016. <http://www.mayoclinic.org/diseases-conditions/malignant-peripheral-nerve-sheath-tumors/basics/definition/con-20035841>.

O'Brien, Michael, Leonard Ahlstrom, and Eddie Carswell. "Somewhere Beyond the Moon." Lyrics. Dimension Music/Stonebrook Music Company, 1996.

For more information contact:

Brenda Lurtey
C/O Advantage Books
P.O. Box 160847
Altamonte Springs, FL 32716

info@advbooks.com

To purchase additional copies of this book visit our bookstore website at: www.advbookstore.com

Longwood, Florida, USA
"we bring dreams to life"™
www.advbookstore.com

CPSIA information can be obtained at www.ICGtesting.com
Printed in the USA
LVOW10s1510260516

490113LV00016B/1066/P